Truth is
Concrete!

3.28.04

SF, CA

911

Truth
Inquiry !!

The Breaking Manager
3 Plays
Sander Hicks

THE BREAKING MANAGER

Three Plays by Sander Hicks

Published Fall 1999 by Soft Skull Press, Inc.

Distributed to the Trade by Consortium.

ISBN 1-887128-37-9

Soft Skull Press

98 Suffolk no. 3A

NYC, NY 10002-3366

www.softskull.com

BACK COVER PHOTO:

Sander on Ludlow

by Gary Hustwit.

The Breaking Light premiered in July of 1998 at the
Ice Factory, New York City with the following cast:

Calculatrice	Emme Shaw
Leonard Kildare	James Urbaniak
Fitz Hirshorn	Sean Gullette
Michael	Joey Golden
Zach	Mark Byrne
Harry	Paul Albe
Daniel McDonagh	Daniel Pardo
Motivational Speaker1	Rosemarie Cepada
Motivational Speaker2	Joyce Lee
Sheryl	Rosemarie Cepada
Tenisha	Joyce Lee
Ben Karadza	Mark Byrne

Directed by Richard Nash.

Sealove, Manager premiered in July of 1997 at the
Ice Factory, New York City with the following cast:

Sealove	Dan O'Brien
Joe Joe	Emily Bank
Mom	Rebecca Nelson
Father Bob	Daniel Pardo
Gary	Jay Snyder
Clerk	Julie Wright
Mr. Klein	John Postley

Directed by Richard Nash.

Rapid City premiered in the Spring of 1996 at
Teatro La Tea, Lower East Side, New York City
with the following cast:

Sealove	Sander Hicks
Lourdes	Carey Cromelin
Zeusie	Todd Colby
Cody	Brent Cox

Directed by Tina Fallon.

FOR RIGHTS TO PRODUCE OR PERFORM THESE PLAYS, PLEASE CONTACT:

Morgan Jenness
Helen Merrill Agency
295 Lafayette Street suite 915
New York, New York 10012-2700
morganjen@aol.com

Dedication

Introduction

by Richard Nash

Hicks throws down the gauntlet.

This statement allows for a variety of interpretations. Logistically these three plays have required me, (as director of the first two plays here) and Tina Fallon (director of *Rapid City*) to:

A) Find a set that can be a garage and a Taco Bell while being sufficiently collapsible to fit in the back of a van;
B) Produce a pop/punk musical with a live band for under a thousand dollars;
C) Stage scenes in cars, a Wal-Mart, a bar, a corporate HQ, and finally, a latter-day storming of the Bastille.

Hicks requires his actors to hold a tomcat's heart in one's hands, run with the dog people, fuck a deer. From the badlands, to the suburbs, to the heart of Capitalism. From the Interstate, to the cul-de-sac, to the corridors of Power.

I talk about challenges because the true challenge facing us as we engage with these plays as a reader and/or audience member is one of faith. By faith I do not mean religion, although the importance of religion to these plays cannot be overstated; so much so that I believe it behooves me to briefly delineate the religious dimension before proceeding to the question of faith.

Hicks's reputation as a political playwright (in the narrow and contemporary sense of "political") can be attributed to the ideological material manifested in an earlier play *Cash Cow* and his most recent *The Breaking Light*. Yet God is quoted more frequently than Marx, Mao, Emma Goldman and the Program of the Revolutionary Communist Party put together!

Look at the plays this way:

The Breaking Light:
The early Christians, taking on the Roman Empire with the power of love.
Sealove, Manager:
The Virgin Mother watching her son debating the Pharisees, leaving home.
Rapid City:
John the Baptist. Mystic. Hallucinating in the desert.

Now, by faith I mean the way in which one lives and expresses belief. Hicks's characters do not simply have a set of cultural or ideological beliefs; they have faith. Incandescent, oscillating on a frequency some can hear, others can't, their faith is our challenge.

Thus the 19th century writer through which I want to talk about these plays is not the "obscure German economist", but Søren Kierkegaard, theologian and existentialist. His dialectical lyric *Fear and Trembling* recounts the story of Abraham obeying God's injunction to sacrifice his only child Isaac whom he loves more than his own life. Abraham chooses to obey, in defiance of any conceivable ethical standard. Kierkegaard holds that it is because of faith: not the faith that God will let him off the hook, for he knows God will not. He knows this, yet at the same time he has faith, on the very strength of the absurdity that a miracle WILL happen, that Isaac will be returned to him. Alternatively that he will be restrained by God from proceeding. "For [Abraham] says, 'Nevertheless [my sacrifice of Isaac] won't happen, or if it does the Lord will give me a new Isaac on the strength of the absurd.'"[1]

Hicks writes plays. Plays are not revolutionary. Once they were and the stories of their lustrous radical past abound: the Astor Place riots over *Hamlet*, Jarry's *Pere Ubu* shouting "Merde" in a crowded theatre, the angry mob at the Abbey Theatre for Synge's *Playboy of the Western World*, the de facto deportation of Malina & Beck of the Living Theatre in the 1960's. But by the late 20th Century the hegemony of Anglo-American culture has rendered us unflappable. In an age where capitalism has embraced Schumpeter's ideal of capitalism as an act of creative destruction, Hicks realizes the only revolution going on is the capitalist revolution, which is capable of absorbing any effort to shock the system through simple co-option. The enzymes of the digestive tract of capitalism are omnivorous. Remain outside the gaping maw as a dissenter and find yourself living as a parasite who cannot survive without its host; the host is happy to let them feed. Thus to believe in the possibility of the revolution is absurd; to think that a play can help is absurder still.

This is true not simply for the playwright himself but for the characters in his plays. Gary, the Werner Erhardt disciple, says "it is time to repair the world," Zeusie tries to be lighter than air, Joe Joe tries to help the Dog people out of the desert to which the fascist bastard fishheads have condemned them, Calculatrice believes that Shitballs will start a revolution. Why? Why will it repair the world, raise Zeusie from the dead, start a revolution?

Why not?

This faith is not learned, nor is it a return to an era of revolution through the levitation of the Pentagon, for Hicks above all is of his generation. To some the politics may be evocative of an earlier generation, but his humanity is of the immediate. As Kierkegaard declares: "However much one generation learns from another, it can never learn from its predecessor the genuinely human factor. In this respect every generation begins afresh, has no task other than that of any previous generation, and comes no further, provided the latter hasn't shirked its task and deceived itself. This authentically human factor is passion.... Thus no generation has learned from another how to love, [and] no generation can begin other than at the beginning."[2]

Hicks, by writing plays, is, in a conventional sense, forgoing his ethical duty to change the world; in effect renouncing the revolution. This is at the core of Kierkegaard's thesis, the "teleological suspension of the ethical,"[3] by which he means: there is an end higher than ethical action. Faith. Hicks retains faith in the miracle, absurd as it seems, that the world will nonetheless be the better for the play. What is astonishing, but ultimately what makes Hicks so important, is that the very absurdity of the faith is the bedrock of the faith. The revolution is impossible. The revolution will prevail. The beauty of his plays is in witnessing the struggle of the women and men of faith against the infidels and the unbelieving world.

Sander Hicks, knight of faith, each play an auto-da-fé, engulfed in fire, signals through the flames.

Richard Nash
May 29th, 1999

1.   Kierkegaard *Fear and Trembling*, trans. Alistair Hannay.
      Penguin. London, 1985. p. 139
2.   ibid., p.145
3.   ibid., p.16

THE BREAKING LIGHT

Calculatrice sitting in the union bar. The slow version of Magazine's "Feed the Enemy" plays on the juke box. Lights come up slowly. She addresses one person in the audience.

Calculatrice   I've been in candy all my life. My parents are from Latvia, donut shop in Baltimore. Became a regular stop with the police. Some high school kids too. I was kind of a fuck-off in high school. I didn't want to be the daughter of the cop-friends. I read Marx, Marcuse, the Panthers, anything I could get my hands on. I got lucky. Transferred schools a couple times in college, couldn't find anything I liked. My parents were supportive. They put it in my head to stick to it, just keep trying. My anger was wearing off. I listened to them. Having a donut shop isn't so horrible, you were giving people something they needed. A smile, a jolt. A better day. I graduated from a little school in Minnesota with a double concentration in sociology and business.

The job market being in a downturn all I could get was entry level in the kitchens at GD Confectionery. Sugar. It's what I knew.

We have a very inclusive union. I made shift manager. I was down there for years. I wasn't always looking to get out but I knew sometime, something would happen. I saw something posted about Marketing. This is when Daniel McDonagh was still head of the department, this is way before the shareholder backlash.

I was this shift leader saying crazy shit about sugar. And here was this guy who unlike everyone else in this goddam company believed in promoting from within. I suggested things at the right time, at first, to just be a fuck off. He incorporated them.

You think things will never change. And then a window opens. That's what I've learned. You have to be alert. Fierce. Let's drink up and hit it. I've got a huge presentation tomorrow.

SCENE ONE – THE PRODUCT PITCH

An Executive Staff Meeting, Boardroom, GD Confectionery Inc.

Calculatrice   Shitballs. What comes to mind?

Leonard   Shit.

Calculatrice   But shit's a bad word. You can't say it on television.

CEO   Surely the product is not shit?

Leonard   Wouldn't, wouldn't surprise me.

Calculatrice   I am pitching you a new product. But what's really at
                    stake here? We create public opinion. I say 'Shitballs.' A
                    little brown candy. With vision. I can make GD
                    Confectionery into a Powerbrand. Shitballs. Profitability
                    in year TWO. Shitballs. A little ball. You pop it into your
                    mouth. It tastes...sweet...yet somehow, more than
                    sweet. It is rich, like foreign chocolate. But also earthy.
                    You break the crusty sugar coating...inside it is moist,
                    warm, dark, it actually reminds you of....

Leonard   Okay, that is IT. I mean I mean you am I the only one
                    the only one here I mean with common sense?
                    Seriously. OK?

Calculatrice   Leonard, who am I really, to this company?

Leonard   The good-looking one up front at the convention, OK?

Calculatrice   Yes, and the youngest. MY generation's mastery of
                    new technology means speed. We can develop this
                    thing in one month.

Leonard   Could I see could I mean what about the market research?

Calculatrice   Punk. Hip Hop. The Drug War. The Gulf War. There's
                    your market research. The new generation is develop-
                    ing in front of our eyes into the supporters of a new

mode of intelligence. This will be expressed in a new form of chocolate. We will supply it. It's not just about sugar anymore. That's Cold War. There more at stake now.

CEO   But I think Leonard had a point. Where's the data that says the market's there.

Calculatrice   Don't think I'm being idealistic.

CEO   We know you're not a, not a, what?

Leonard   Bomb-thrower.

Calculatrice   You called me that last time. I'm glad we value creativity here.

Leonard   Return on investment. The shareholders just want R-O-I, honey. They don't care what names we call each other.

Calculatrice   I don't place a premium on the present. I develop markets. I'm in the future. Who's in?

Leonard   We're out of our scheduled time.

Calculatrice   Stop putting up walls. Let's build the team. Mr. Vice President, I don't want to make it seem like we're in the new paradigm without you.

Leonard   I'm supportive of the new technologies.

Calculatrice   I believe you. Shitballs. Say it. Say yes. Vote yes. Your own fears keep you back.

CEO   Hmm. Well we've got a lot to think about, don't we? Maybe something a little more, with those random features, sort of a one-in-five chance this version of the product will appear adapted in a special way for the purchaser? Why Shitballs? Why now? Will it sell in Dubuque? Could you get back to me on that? I think you're doing a great job. But you're going to need to get everyone's buy-in. I think you know that. Hey. Thank You. OKAY.

SCENE TWO – EMPTY CARS OUT ON THE HIGHWAY

Michael and Zach in a car, Zach is driving.

Michael   I want the hotels to be bigger. I want the audiences to
                 be smarter.

Zach   You speak in any hotel.

Michael   I speak in any hotel on the itinerary.

Zach   I drive. With directions. That are often outdated.

Michael   And you sell books and tapes. Which you know is prob-
                 ably more important.

Zach   I'm happy with both jobs. I like the highway.

Michael   The hotels could be larger.

Zach   You speak in any hotel on the itinerary.

Michael   What is the limit? Do I look outside? No. I look inside
                 first. The hotels are a certain size. What is inside me
                 that lets me let the Party book us in small and medium
                 size hotels?

Zach   You're eager to speak in any hotel.

Michael   That's right. That's right.

Zach   Can't you resign yourself to your present point in histo-
                 ry and in the history of your life?

Michael   Never stop. The struggle is never over. No one stops.
                 Nothing stops and is measurable.

Zach   I think this engine has a bent valve.

Michael   How can you tell?

Zach	A little thooping sound I hear sometimes.
Michael	How much is this going to cost to fix
Zach	It's like throwing a rod. You might as well swap out the entire engine.
Michael	Oh that would be just lovely. Can you imagine getting them to write a check for that?
Zach	I know.
Michael	"I'm a revolutionary and a member of an organization, but I am also the Treasurer. I would pay that expense, but I'm too fraught with contradictions. Plus, the corporations didn't pay us for you on time this month so there's no money."
Zach	Hitchhiker. Do you want to stop?
Michael	Somebody in worse shape. This should be a nice mix.
Zach	I think we should stop.
Michael	I'm not your leader.

They stop and back up to the hitchhiker.

Michael	How far you goin?
Harry	Pretty far.
Michael	Good. You like to talk politics?

SCENE THREE – PRIVATE PITCH

Later. Calculatrice and CEO Fitz Hirschorn are alone at the conference table.

Calculatrice	Well?

CEO	It's risky. Shitballs. Shitballs.
Calculatrice	Fitz, those first month sales reports are going to hit us Fed Ex after the first of the month. You will open them and go right to the bottom line. Spelled out, in black and white, will be the cracked code, the mathematics of aggression.
CEO	You're going to have to guarantee the financial people Return on Investment.
Calculatrice	A brand is a promise. A promise is all about the future.
CEO	Where did you learn how to hypnotize people? Graduate school?
Calculatrice	I'm in touch with my personal power.
CEO	Is there a generation gap here, or do I just think I'm understanding you and really the words don't mean what I think you're meaning, but they come together right, and I love to hear them.
Calculatrice	The realm of ideas dominates the real world.
CEO	You have my support, in theory. Business is all about taking risks. My job is to manage the risks.
Calculatrice	I want Leonard to understand. Why does he refuse to get it?
CEO	Understand Leonard responded out of fear.
Calculatrice	I've eradicated all the fear from my life. Why can't he? I appreciate Leonard's fears. I also reserve the right to ignore them. My business mentor, Daniel McDonagh taught me you ignore the data you're not looking for. Paint the picture the shareholders bought, right?
CEO	As CEO, my primary task is to add shareholder value.
Calculatrice	Or create the appearance of added value

CEO	There's truth in appearances?
Calculatrice	It's the skin of the truth. The cool surface tension.
CEO	I hope "Shitballs" can captivate the market the way the skin of the truth does. I'm going to reserve decision until after the Executive Hunting Trip. But I want you out there with us. You know how to load a kalashnikof?
Calculatrice	Of course.
CEO	You belong on board.
Calculatrice	Hegel said the Mind is the only thing real. And there's only one thing the Mind ever really thinks about: freedom.
CEO	Understand, it's important to stay in touch with the raw essence. Get out of the suits and see who we really are. Build the team. Everything will be handled with the greatest of taste.
Calculatrice	Let's wrap up.
CEO	Thumbs up, thumbs down?
Calculatrice	I'll email you once I've checked my e-mail.

she turns to go.

CEO	Hey
Calculatrice	Yes?
CEO	You have my cell.
Calculatrice	Yes.
CEO	You're gonna call me.
Calculatrice	OK.

CEO	what?
Calculatrice	Yes.

beat.

CEO	Thanks.

SCENE FOUR – UNDER THE BRIGHT LIGHTS

Michael, Zach and Harry walking through the various sections of a Wal-Mart, starting out in Automotive.

Harry	It might not a bent valve then, it could be just the carburetor manifolds. The pipes that hold that sucker on.
Zach	That would be wonderful.
Harry	I've sometimes seen it where you can secure the carb manifolds with plumbing hose clamps.
Zach	You are truly saving us.
Harry	Only Jesus can truly save you.
Zach	Oh really? How much does that cost?

beat.

Harry	You thought it was a whole new engine. I'm telling you you're much closer.
Michael	Look at this mass-produced cheap wonderfulness. And yet the designs are wanting. Why are the beautifully designed objects in the lives of the rich?
Harry	They have better taste.
Michael	They have better things. Why do we get the blunt,

ugly, heavy things? Most people live with the shoddy and disposable.

Harry   America has a free market that finds the best and sup-
               ports it. You have a world of variety so that the good
               stuff can win and survive. They call it Market
               Discipline. You atheists have no sense of excellence.
               No taste. No sense of the Divine.

Michael   Market Discipline finds the best and reserves it for
               those you can pay the best price. So yes, you have
               excellence, but the people who own the machines that
               made it keep it

Harry   You sound like an anarchist. Have you ever met a Real
               Christian?

Michael   Let's agree: people live degraded lives.

Harry   If they choose to.

Michael   Degraded by their jobs, their bosses, or you might
               say, their sins. Believe me, I have a sense of the
               divine. But the worst thing is, people get degraded
               because they adapt to it. We accept bad design,
               because daily we are in contact with fear. It's the same
               fear that guides an industry to be "safe" and "normal"
               in designing, ...coffee mugs, for instance. A lack of
               vision keeps the best design for coffee mugs out of
               the hands of the masses, because the industries aren't
               guided by a mission to improve life. They were taught
               to make a profit now, sell coffee mugs. Someday peo-
               ple will really look at their lives, look at their coffee
               mugs, and at all the objects in their life, and suddenly
               see the mediocrity, the inferiority of these objects. If
               that happens, I think they will be angry.

Harry   But who decides what is good design?

Michael   Design is all about solving problems. It is the struggle
               of people to live in a problematic world. There are
               standards. To doubt the existence of at least some
               standard is to wander into a swamp.

Harry	But whose standard?
Michael	Exactly. That of the rich? The poor? The suburban?
Harry	Hegel said the only thing real is the Mind. And the Mind really only thinks about one thing: God.
Michael	But whose god? That of the rich? The poor?
Harry	Oh, the rich and the poor are in the same boat. God isn't owned by anyone. He is not over the world, but springs out from within it.
Michael	Tony the Tiger. For Frosted Flakes. God is just a mascot of the guiding truths of a particular culture. A personification.
Harry	Have you read any of the twentieth century Christian Apologetics?
Michael	No.
Harry	Neither have most people. It's new Christianity. It is not the enemy of reason, or rationality, but asks, where does Reason come from? The origin of Reason points back towards the existence of the divine. They say if God and the supernatural do not exist, neither can Reason.

beat.

Michael	You get what you're looking for.

They are in the hardware section.

Harry	General-use hose clamps. Just what your clunker needs. I found what we are all searching for. Someone's looking out for us. This warrants going a couple extra miles in my shoes. Right?
Zach	Right.

Calculatrice in her office.

Calculatrice I am hunting. This is a picture of me, hunting. Orange cap. Long rifle. Scope. Crosshairs. Sitting in a shack in thirty degrees for four hours. Smelling the air. I imagine Leonard having sex with the cold, dead animals in a field of dry winter grass. The CEO finds him in his cross hairs. I am watching. This is me watching. I give a little nod. Squeeze, Fitz. "Bomb-thrower?" Coward. He doesn't know how professional I can be. I will do anything to advance my career in this Corporation. I am a virtuous person and I am hunting. I see a deer. It's not dead. It's warm blooded. It is in line with my virtue. It wants me. I am a physical, emotional, strong person holding a long rifle. What if this deer was something I truly wanted? What if I slept with this deer with no strings attached, but allowing anything to happen. It's important to retain spontaneity. Eventually you realize you can do anything, that you will do anything to advance, and what you do is what comes natural. That you are guided by instinct and virtue at the same time. In this organization, it's my duty to keep the blood flowing. We're not going to ossify, bewildered at the transformative speeds of the new technologies. I AM SPEED. Squeeze, Fitz. I personify the new freedom. If I get off on the violation of my "personal" ethics, it might do wonders for my career. Tantalizing. Like a deer in the woods. With its nose in the air, trying to find me...Daniel.

Daniel Calculatrice.

Calculatrice Can I get you something?

Daniel I'm a dead man. I work dawn to midnight now. You haven't stopped by yet. I thought I'd see you.

Calculatrice CEO. I heard. I'm so proud.

Daniel A CEO is nothing but a manager.

Calculatrice	You are the source of the Company's spirit. You have to inspire them. Power is question of very material forces.
Daniel	That's just politics. Power is an obligation.
Calculatrice	It's good to see you. I need you.
Daniel	I realize I over-reacted. I'm happy now. The Shareholders spoke. That's it. OK.
Calculatrice	They blundered. I've got a new product I'm pitching. This is it. You'd recognize it. It's going to put us on the map.
Daniel	I want to talk to you about it.
Calculatrice	Then why do you ignore my email.
Daniel	It's hard to explain. When I was your boss I wanted so many times to kiss you. But I always felt like you felt I was more of a father to you. Plus I was your boss.
Calculatrice	And my mentor.
Daniel	I'm in therapy now. It's been advised that I ask you if you are interested in initiating a relationship with me.
Calculatrice	Oh, how sweet.
Daniel	Well, I have to go.
Calculatrice	Wait. I'd like to show you how I'm projecting this.
Daniel	You're head of the department now.
Calculatrice	Hey, you can't come and go as you please here. You don't have access.
Daniel	You're going to pull rank on me? I got you into this department. You got into this business wanting to burn it down.

Calculatrice	You have to see this formula before you go. It will make you afraid of me.
Daniel	I don't know how you feel.
Calculatrice	The same qualities that make a you leader, an executive, make you impossible to be close to. To be friends with anyone really, especially the people you work with.
Daniel	(Points) You're not looking at yourself first. And at this moment, you've got a little fire to put out in your own office. Good luck.

Daniel exits, and from opposite direction, on comes Leonard, dragging a long 11x14 spindled fanfold paper printout.

Leonard	Calculatrice. I was just ON-LINE. I was just on the INTERNET. OK? I saw the First Year Sales projections? What is this, your personality expressed in spread-sheets?
Calculatrice	I never stop. Do you like it?
Leonard	You can't do that. No final right hand column. You can't just have no conclusion.
Calculatrice	No one ever trained you to be bold.
Leonard	This new products proposal is bloated with half-truths, grease. It's a rope bridge. It's candy and charms and I don't even like candy. OK?
Calculatrice	You're pulling us back.
Leonard	Seek to understand, then to be understood.
Calculatrice	This isn't about the proposal. We all know the spread-sheet is a projection! What's a projection? Light on a wall. Cute that I can program the file to go on to infinity, as if business never changes. But it does. And people get changed, or they change first. It's hard. Are you going on the executive hunting trip Leonard?

Leonard	"Are you going on the executive hunting trip Leonard," what is that OK?
Calculatrice	I am. Looks like we're both executives now. That's hard for you, you think I'm a pretty face with a big mouth. But I want to ask you a question as if we were friends.
Leonard	A real officer of the Corporation doesn't try to make friends. A real officer simply attempts to increase shareholder value. What's the question?
Calculatrice	Shitballs!
Leonard	Do you think I'm retarded?
Calculatrice	If you don't want to be friends, I will be forced to take you for a ride. The new generation does not fear the scatological. My gut tells me we're ready for a product packaging of the daily soil that moves us. We like shit. We're born into middle class sterility and we find ways to subvert it. Let go. Once I was young and stubborn and guided by voices that said there would never be a place for me at the top of this machine. But now I've got a job that rewards my boldness. Do you know what intransigent means? You've found a place you like and you're not moving. You're a vapor. This is my office.

Leonard exits. She muses.

Shit. To shit. We shit. Is there a better word for it? There is none. It's the low-end vernacular we're going with, any other word for it is either high-end medical or cartoon-level stupid. It's time to redeem the vernacular. This is real democracy.

Harry, Michael and Zach are rebuilding the carb. Parts are everywhere. Harry is the most coated in grease.

Harry	So. You're a communist, aren't you?
Michael	Yes. I'm several things.
Harry	I knew it. Talking about people that way. There's not too many communists left.
Michael	I'm also a motivational speaker.
Harry	Motivational speaker, eh?
Michael	We were on our way to our next engagement. Daniel McDonagh's upstart cola company. A real challenger to the Coke monopoly. Kind of radical. I mean, in a capitalist sort of way. You think we can get back on the road by sundown?
Harry	Have faith
Michael	I do.
Harry	I suppose I'd rather I got picked up by a communist than some of these surface Christians...What do you speak about?
Michael	Principles. What life is worth living for. What it's worth getting motivated about. America has a long tradition of self-help books. From Ben Franklin to...well, Most of it's about the ego, about psyching yourself up to do things in a heightened, aggressive state. No underlying principles to justify this ego-trip work ethic. They perpetuate the fragmented thinking of big business, the breaking light of the end of an era. Hard to see clear.
Harry	Uh-huh.

Zach	I can imagine this engine purring. Have you ever thought of blending Christianity and Marxism?
Harry	You'd end up with neither.
Michael	But what about a blend of Marxism and management theory?
Zach	Sometimes I wonder if God does exist, but not in the way the ruling class teaches. If He does exist, as the essence of all that is good, of all that is true.
Harry	Yeah.
Zach	But how can you prove this?
Michael	Why? What for? Ask yourself, why bother looking for an embodiment of these things? Why not just accept the concrete truths as they are, and go with them?
Harry	You can't prove He exists. He exists for me in a place over reason and proofs. How can you use reason to prove the source of all reason?...What is a proof?
Michael	The source of scientific law.
Harry	And how is it proven?
Michael	Through experience. Through empirical observation of experience.
Harry	So, science is all just what has happened before.
Michael	Yes, precedent.
Harry	But what about what hasn't happened yet? The realm of things independent of the past. Not hinged on what has happened. God exists in the realm of the possible. God exists and science is puny in comparison. Science lives in the past.
Zach	That makes a lot of sense, actually.

Michael	What? Nobody WANTS to live in the past. I used to hear this stuff all the time back in California.
Harry	The New Age is bankrupt. But the Old Testament is alive and well.
Michael	the oppressed wandering Jews needed a morale boost. A mascot. a strong father figure with a bad personality....
Harry	Excuse me. Excuse me. There are plenty of imperfect religions to mock. What you are calling the "personality" of God is human culture.
Michael	The culture is the values is the style that those people needed 4,000 years ago because they were starving.
Harry	You're looking at it backwards. What would Hegel say? He'd ask you what is it that drives human history?

Harry pulls the cracked carbourator manifolds out of the engine. He holds them up to the light.

	What's the engine look like? Does the engine not exist? Yet the car moves fast. The people are starving in the desert, yet they are the divine chosen people.
Michael	Coincidence?
Harry	They survived is the miracle. What is the cause of it all, throughout history, what is the source of things happening? Where do the ideas come from? Space? Rationalists cough God away and dismiss the pictures, they blow their arrogant noses at the imagery they take for God. That's a quick way out. I think you have a head on your shoulders, I think you can do better. You say you're a communist, well that kind of arrogance doesn't serve the people. I should write a book on motivating communists. My son's a communist.
Michael	I am motivated. I am a motivational speaker.
Harry	Have you read Isaiah?

Michael   Have you read Mao?

Harry   "The Lord rises to accuse

                 standing to try his people

                 The Lord enters into judgements

                 with his people's elders and princes

                 It is you who have devoured the vineyard

                 the loot wrested from the poor is in your houses.

                 What do you mean by crushing my people

                 and grinding down the poor when they look at you?"

Michael   THAT's in the Bible?

Harry hands Michael his Bible, grease proof in its plastic binder.

Harry   "So says the Lord the God of Hosts."

Michael   Or, so says the poor and the pissed-off who wrote that.

Harry   You think you invented the idea of Justice. You commu-
                 nists come out of the city with your big words and you
                 pointy noses but you don't read. You think you're above
                 the one book that itself authored 4000 years of society
                 and Law. You think revolution is going to be authored by
                 you? You all couldn't motivate the Russian factory work-
                 ers to go beyond narrow self-interest! What a no-brainer!

Michael   Russia had no history of motivational self-help literature.

Harry grabs the new hose clamps and installs them.

                 America already knows revolution. You all aren't teach-
                 ing anything new. America is a holy land. And will

become holier. The revolution is always a holy act. Just like it is written in Isaiah, one man stands up and predicts divine justice. The nobles and elders have led the people astray, but Justice will sweep through us like a storm from our of nowhere out on the South Dakota prairie. Babylon falls, it always does, in time. "The arrogant will be laid low...The idols will perish forever...on that day men will throw to the moles and the bats the idols of silver and gold which they made for worship." What can you say to that.

Michael   "Cast away illusions. Prepare for Struggle."

Harry   Amen. Let me know when you finish the book of Isaiah. You want to meet the real revolution? I'll introduce you to him.

SCENE SEVEN – THE PROXY AND THE ROBOT

Leonard   Fitz!

CEO   I am not Hirshhorn. I am the proxy of CEO Fitz Hirshhorn. I look just like him.

Leonard   Er.

CEO   Like the Japanese say.

Leonard   What?

CEO   Always deal through intermediaries.

Leonard   Yes. Right. What is the the the I mean what is the the. Message?

CEO   Dissatisfaction. The CEO and staff are concerned about your adaptability to new products, new technologies.

Leonard	I LOVE the new technologies. I love the new technologies. Love, OK?
CEO	Love is not living. You have to live the new technologies. Business is changing. Keep up or be made the symbol of a sloth. This is a performance counseling statement. I'm going to ask you to sign it.

Leonard reads.

CEO	I have no leisure time in this schedule.
Leonard	I've got a family!

He signs and turns to dash off.

CEO	One last thing. You've lost gun privileges on the Hunting Trip.

SCENE EIGHT – ON THE HUNTING TRIP

CEO & Calculatrice holding long rifles

CEO	What do we need?
Calculatrice	Vision.
CEO	We have vision. We need motivation.
Calculatrice	Motivational speakers are like emotional cops. The people who work for you shouldn't have their emotions regulated.
CEO	There are no private affairs, here, we're all on company time. We care, maybe too much. We pay you an executive salary. We need to guarantee you're motivated.
Leonard	My department is more than willing to fund a new source of motivation.

Calculatrice	Fitz, we'd be better off if we wrote the program our-selves. Us three could do a better job then some street preacher.
Leonard	We're talking professionals here, miss. I happen to own a copy of the corporate motivational trainers index, OK? Cross-classified by subject, background and fee. We can find one to suit our needs. (To Calculatrice.) This, ma'am, is what you call being pro-active.
Calculatrice	Actually, sir, the original definition of proactive is when you realize your ability to choose a response to any given stimuli. Don't confuse it with initiative. Everyone does. What you're doing is just Active.
CEO	Look it up. And Leonard, do this, but get us someone for a reasonable fee. Calculatrice, you said the realm of ideas dominates the real world.
Calculatrice	It depends on which ideas.
CEO	Leonard, bring in a range of candidates. Now then. He loads his rifle. Let's kills something. Calculatrice dar-ling, remember to aim for the heart. Piercing the less-er organs ruins the meat.

Michael and Daniel, in bar.

Michael   I've read all about you. "The Underground Coke." It was an honor addressing your company....

Daniel   Cap it. This place is full of monkeys. They all are. They're all built on myth. You smile and play the game. What can I get you.

Michael   I'll have a bourbon and soy milk if they have it. So. What keeps you going, if you don't believe in this place.

Daniel   Inertia. I made CEO at 35. I'm not sure at this point what more there is. Do you have kids.

Michael   My brother has kids.

Daniel   You can't understand. You want to be a good dad someday? You have to lie to them about Santa Claus.

Michael   Well you could say okay here it is it's Christmas, and parents like to give their children gifts on Christmas. Instead of perpetuating the lie.

Daniel   Disregarding your own self-indulgent honesty, what's the harm in the myth?

Michael   You're teaching my kids manipulation.

Daniel   Myth is a two-way street. The kids want to buy into it. There are prizes.

Michael   Prizes.

Daniel   You might find yourself in a less self-righteous moment in the future, with children, knowing time is short, and most of their lives will not be spent with you. You might want to bring the magic of this world to them. They aren't gullible as much as just willing to believe. And not just because of the prizes, but because of the magic.

Michael's beeper goes off. He checks it.

That's what capitalism is built on: The Splash. The SIZZLE. The Magic mutually agreed to. It's not built on the backs of workers, give me a break, workers are actually quite smart. I know some. I honestly do. Do you? We build capitalism out of dreams, sacrifice, risk. Robert Guizzetto, CEO of coke, took their stock from 4 billion to 70 billion in his 15 years at the top.

Michael   I thought you were sick of the corporations.

Daniel   I run one. I'm just sick of this one. I'm ambitious because of a very deep hole inside me. OK? I'm Santa Claus. I'm the product of vision: In 1904 you didn't have Santa Claus. You had a moldering St. Nicholas legend and a cola company in love with the color red. Put them together and blammo. Santa Claus was born. He was mass-produced. The technology of printing, printing on beverage trays, in the Saturday Evening Post, printing, Coca Cola ads printed created Santa Claus. Don't tell me you don't respect that.

Michael   I'm getting beeped for a job.

Daniel   HEY THANKS FOR THE DRINK.

SCENE TEN – THANK YOU WE'LL CALL: AUDITIONING THE MOTIVATIONALS

Calculatrice and CEO with rifles, on Hunting Trip.

Leonard   Thanks for coming on such short notice. What's your core motivational theory?

Motivational#1 It's the theory of "Outgoing Message". It's a theory, and a pun. Your practice of management won't be principled or mission-driven without the right "Outgoing Message" on your voice mail. If your "Outgoing Message" isn't truly "outgoing", then you yourself will not be "outgoing."

Leonard   I'll keep that in mind. Thank you. Fire.

Calculatrice and CEO open fire. Motivational#1 is dead.

Leonard   Next.

Motivational#2   My theory of manager motivation blends the best of the French Postmoderns, everyone from the deconstructionists to the information society mavericks. Over drinks, I once told Jean Baudrillard, "nothing is real unless it is reproducible, and nothing is as real as its copies and reproductions." He wrote that down and made his reputation. So my theory is that a truly postmodern manager will have no originality, but will motivate her staff based on gross appropriation and reproduction of others' thoughts.

Leonard   Cute. Very up to the minute. Open fire.

They fire.

Calculatrice   Now wait, aren't we creating more demand for bad motivational speakers by winnowing the supply?

CEO   Calc, this is the Free Market. I'm not interested in Supply and Demand of inferior product. I support excellence. Lock and load.

They reload. Enter Michael.

Leonard   What's *your* theory?

Michael   I love that question. How much time do I have?

Leonard   Just gimmie the gimmick.

Michael touches his chin. He takes a second

Michael   You are the business class. The leaders of industry. Yet the changing pace of business demands that we adapt. An obscure German economist once said that when technology changes, the way we relate changes. Who learns this first? Those working with the technologies. In a more industrial field, this would be the workers on the machines. When it applies to business technologies, then it's you. The business class, the leaders of industry. What is your dominant social relation? Carpe Diem. Exploit the moment. And the resources. Am I right? This shows a lot of spine on your part. Why you make what you make, right? But we've already said that technology changes the social relations. So what is the new social relation going to be? Let's back up and make sure we're all on the same page. You.

Points to Leonard.

Help me out y'all. What ARE the "new technologies?"

Leonard	Um.
Michael	Hit me.
Leonard	E-E-mail?
Michael	OK, email. That's one. Anymore? Anybody else?
Calculatrice	It was a trick question!
Michael	No it wasn't.
Calculatrice	E-mail is only an immediate result of a changing technological paradigm.
Michael	Well, OK, that's right. The real motivational instigators are the new values. The digital age increases the speed of business. But speed is just the tip of the iceberg. Information storage is decentralized. Small machines have been mass-produced and distributed. People can know more, and have more power. But information, networked intelligence, all the gadgets are again, just the indicators of an new improved social structure. With real democratic potential. And this gets us to the core of the

motivations: the basic masses. They're who we are really in business for, right? To serve the needs of the customers, the ones poised for the new power in this new epoch, right, the ones with needs they don't yet know how to satisfy? Am I right here? Sir, as CEO, what's your primary task?

CEO   Um.

Michael   Yes?

CEO   It's not.

Michael   It's not, yes, please.

CEO   I was trained....

Michael   Ye....

CEO   ...To say...

Michael   The basic masses am I right? And by that I mean the customers, the consumers?

CEO   As CEO, my primary task is to add shareholder value.

beat.

               But I've enjoyed your talk on the new technologies so far, and am waiting for the motivation part. I hope I haven't thrown you off.

Michael   Shareholder value. Yes. All power to the owners. A corporation beholden to the bottom line, to a mass of profit-driven value-interested shareholders.

CEO   Like I said, I didn't mean...

Michael   We can't let this culture limit our reality. The French don't run business beholden to the shareholders. Neither do the Japanese. There's more to life than profits. There's more at stake. Right?

Calculatrice	New values.
Michael	Exactly.
Calculatrice	We all know a culture is nothing but the expression of values.
Michael	And those values are about freedom, or they are not. You have to make a break with history if you're really seeking transformation.
Calculatrice	Hegel said the Mind is essentially about one thing.
Michael	Freedom.
Calculatrice	Freedom!
Michael	(*to CEO*) A firm grasp on the new values impacted by the technologies inevitably leads to higher profits, good morale, a winning organization and satisfied shareholders. 'Cause we know that crowd can get skittish, right?
CEO	Like cattle!!
Michael	Let's break and move to small groups!

He and Calculatrice move off stage to a private caucus.

SCENE ELEVEN – GRUMPY BEAR LOST IN THE WOODS

Leonard	Can you believe some of this?
CEO	It's vaguely West-Coast. They had a guy like this at the Convention.
Leonard	It's not just his style. You know what I think?
CEO	Could you just tell me?

Leonard	Three words: Bomb-thrower. OK?
CEO	Well, it's a lot of theory right now.
Leonard	It's a lot of hot air...that smells.
CEO	Maybe we can just use what we want. How much was he?
Leonard	Well what the hell I mean what are we supposed to be doing right now?
CEO	Writing a personal mission statement.
Leonard	NOBODY BELIEVES MISSION STATEMENTS.

SCENE TWELVE – SYNTHESIS

Michael	Well maybe its time to move on. Is it all about things to own? Art? Businesses? My mission is to create an effective strategy for those who have been supporting this system with their broken backs. Those who work seething, always hearing about the things the bosses value, own, want. The unhappiness is the guarantee. Justice and history are living masses of life. They need exercise, turnover. Two centuries ago the aristocracy was overthrown by the bourgeoisie. Today, that bourgeoisie has become a dictatorship. More powerful than the old aristocracy, look at this country. We have had presidents say their primary task is to keep this country a place where anyone can become rich. The perfect expression of the bourgeois ideal.
Calculatrice	And it's two-hundred years old.
Michael	wearing thin.
Calculatrice	My department here at GD Confectionery is already pretty focused on some pretty revolutionary values. We're having a hard time getting everyone to understand them

though. Tomorrow is not pretty. I'm not interested in good taste.

Michael   You have to know how to sell it to them. You have to put it in language they'll understand. These executives also need to be able to believe in it. Although I think the impulses towards democracy will ultimately strip them of their power. Why Marketing? Don't you think you should be higher up in the leadership here?

Calculatrice   Maybe

Michael   You think new, evolutionary, futuristic so called egalitarian values expressed in products is enough?

Calculatrice   Well, how far are you willing to go?

Michael   Pretty far.

Calculatrice   Marketing is one place in capitalist production that supports dialogue on principles.

Michael   Well, how far are you willing to go?

Calculatrice   I used to be anarchist. But I like the world of business because it values certainty. Or is that the illusion we get sucked in by.

Michael   Wishy-washy relativism is everywhere. It means you don't know. And the rich love it, they want not to be judged. But even the Bible predicts there will be justice someday. I'm not saying...well, it is in there. Have you read Isaiah? It's incredible.

Calculatrice   Isaiah? Like in the Bible?

Michael   *It is you who have devoured the vineyard*
The loot wrested from the poor is in your houses....
What do you mean by crushing the poor
when they look up at you?

It's a question of finding the right text, the right values, and creating a revolution. We both believe consciousness can change the world.

Calculatrice   We are walking tightropes here. It leads you not to trust anyone.

Michael   Look at them. All with an eye out back for the back stab. Does it have to be autocratic commanding? Real leadership instigates change. Inspirational force. I love people, but not everyone has the talent to lead a revolution. You have that potential. I think you should take it seriously.

Calculatrice   Look at them. Scratching their fat necks.

Michael   Ask yourself: do you want power?

Calculatrice   *(Looking at them.)*
Yes.

Michael   Then decide to take power. You have an advantage when you're not guided by self-interest. You'll triumph when you become guided by the desire to do for other people. You suddenly have a will not your own will, but the sum of the wills of all those who work here. Look at them, Calculatrice. Do they think of the broken backs they're standing on? Do they speak like you can? Fire them. The new technologies have opened up a window for new values. Take people through.

SCENE 13 – DROPPING THE GAUNTLET

Calculatrice   I propose we move towards a vote, closure. The debate's gone on long enough. It's Shitballs manufactured under this production schedule or I seriously question the ability of this company to look forward. Let's keep in mind the core values of Leonard's motivational speaker.

Leonard   He wasn't...um...OK? Let me make one thing perfectly clear. He they said he wasn't supposed to just I didn't Jesus.

a little beat.

Calculatrice   The people are looking towards corporate America for leadership. Where will the new values find a home? Let's do it. Shitballs. For the American People.

Leonard   Do you ever get the feeling none of this is actually happening? You blame yourself for having a slippery grip on reality, but then you say, I never asked for this life. I would kill for a dry martini. The direction New Products has taken recently has left me dizzy. I'm going to throw up I'm so dizzy. Yes, there are new technologies. Do they change everything immediately? No. There are still fundamental issues of right and wrong, it's okay to call yourself a conservative if you're talking about business. I thought we all agreed. There's likewise a natural respect for language that prevents us from considering the Director of Marketing's New Products proposal. OK?

Calculatrice   You're VP of Finance. You're out of your department addressing issues concerning language.

Leonard   I know what's right.

Calculatrice   I've got profitability in year two. Address that.

Leonard   We've got other products to defend. Guaranteed money-makers.

Calculatrice   The other products keep this company making money in its sleep. I'm talking about new cashflow. Liquidity power that will let this company lash out and sting, an elasticity, a sweet, razor-point position. 18% increased market share.

Leonard   According to your spreadsheet.

Calculatrice   I really feel like I'm holding your hand. Did you have a deficiency of love in your childhood?

CEO   "Criticize performance, not people."

Leonard   Fitz, come on, what do you think?

CEO

He takes a second, then slowly, fatalistically, fatherly

> She's got profitability in year two.

SCENE FOURTEEN – BACK ON THE ROAD

Zach driving Harry and Michael again.

Michael   Let's sum-up. What's the destiny of this country?

Harry   To become a holy land.

Michael   Wait

Harry   Babylon will fall, it is hollow. A government based on holiness will replace it.

Michael   What is holiness?

Harry   The presence of God.

Michael   What is God?

Harry   There is no idea of justice without him. That's why communism only looks good on paper. Do you want to be stuck just reading things that are only 100 years old? Jesus Christ came to save the poor. We are all poor.

Michael   Harry, I can see how there's been nothing in this culture to reinforce these noble intentions of yours, so you turn to religion. But the core principles of your God exist independently of the religions of the rich. You don't have to have anything in common with them. As you continue traveling with us, I hope we can show you that. That's our practice. Practice, study, practice. Be ready for anything.

Harry

Who's recruiting who? Your heart's in the right place, but you can't see the glass when it's right in front of your nose.

Michael

It looks like we got the contract at GD Confectionary. We are going to motivate the entire executive staff and the workforce in the physical plant. I want you to help us. Talking about values leads to real social justice.

Harry

If you want justice in this world, you're going to have to read more. Not just the stuff the Party gives you.

Michael

I read Isaiah when you gave it to me. It changed me. What did you think of Mao's Yenan Conference speech on culture?

Harry

I didn't read it.

Michael

I don't think that's fair.

Harry

Nothing's fair in this world. I don't know why you want to be my friend.

Michael

Real revolution won't ever happen in this country unless we share the texts that burn like watchfires. You and I are sentries. You're a Christian. I'm a Communist. But we've got to build some bridges.

Harry

America's closer to me than to you. I like you, but there's nothing compelling me towards sticking around. I think it's time to stop talking and do something. I'll be getting off at the next truck stop.

Zach

But the engine is purring.

Harry

And I wish you all luck. I hope you find what you're looking for. I really do.

Speaking into a dictaphone.

ZACH   By time you hear this we will have gone farther than any of you. We will be beyond recall by the Central Committee. But we feel we are learning a lot about Christianity and Corporate America, and haven't strayed from the secret goals of the party. We wanted to get this out to you in case anything happens. Something is going to happen. The signs are there. Oh, and we got the contract at GD.

In the short time I have, I bring you news from the road. We all agreed the leadership of the Party needed fresh blood. We all agreed last time the Party hadn't done anything new in years and that maybe we had been acting purely out of habit for too long. So you sent us out to study all of those god damn How-To-Self-Help MANAGEMENT books. And now we're motivational speakers. Thanks. You wouldn't believe the decadence. But there is hope. In the brittle branches of the bourgeoisie, there's one person that makes this kamikaze mission worthwhile. She's what we are looking for. She's in the Union. She's read Hegel. She is fire.

According to Lenin, we know that the vanguard leadership of the Party must ultimately come from the working class, not white collar crime. And this party sprang from the New Left of the 60's, where Students for a Democratic Society defined the working class broadly, encompassing academics and intellectuals. Define it broadly goddamit. It is broad. The owners are few and well-protected.

This is a schizophrenic country. Most people tell you their story; their class identity is this constantly shifting thing. We have to get in touch with the true class nature of this society: schizophrenia. As part of our research I have unearthed the following facts: in 1850, 75% of the USA lived on a farm. Today, that majority has moved to the cities. Whatever class you're in, the basis of the history of most families goes back only a generation or two to an agrarian, close-to-the-land consciousness. This history is our destiny. It's what's built into the national subconscious. So the schizophrenia is founded on a very organic populist farming consciousness. Can we rely on that when push comes to shove?

If you feel we're talking too many risks, are moving too fast, are being ultraleft, suicidal terrorist middle-class left-adventurists, then send us a wire. But you're going to have to get it into the compound at GD on foot. Cause we've gone pretty far in.

We will do everything we can. We can only do what we can. We are advancing towards the light. Look at the seven principles from the April victory brainstorm. Trust we are serving the ultimate goals of the Party. Trust us to drop the hammer when the time is right. Trust we are shaping and sharpening people's minds to eradicate the dog eat dog fuck you system forever.

The struggle's never over.

He turns the dictaphone off.

Amen.

SCENE SIXTEEN – YOU CAN GO YOUR OWN WAY

Harry   Without God, you don't address Man's sinfulness. The
                  revolution is cursed to become totalitarian.

Michael   What is the destiny of this country?

Harry   To become a just land.

Michael   Because we agree this country's destiny is not fate,
                  but its history.

Harry   America is only a half-built place.

Michael	Nice. I think since it is half-built, it itself is inherently totalitarian. The rich run everything. Electoral politics elect the rich! The ballot box has never stopped them. It has never secured us against the boom/bust economy. Every fews years another war. The media create a smokescreen. Totalitarian power pulses under the skin of the animal.
Harry	But what are you going to do about it?
Michael	The schisms of this system are floating out there. You and I and the Party are going to drive a wedge. The owners won't know what hit them, or where the force is originating from. From the country they have forsaken, their cities will be invaded. By the truth, the concrete of the country.
Harry	I'm just a hitchhiker. I'm not a member of any group. You all have stopped moving.
Michael	Mao called for the constant revolutionizing of the Party, so we won't become totalitarian. The dictatorship of the proletariat is true democracy, but it would take me days to explain it.
Harry	Well, my bags are already packed.
Michael	The dictatorship of the proletariat is only a transitional phase. It took me years to get it. I understand...Oh, don't get out of the car now.
Harry	Look a motel. Hey listen fellas. It's been a journey, OK? You never walk alone. I'll pray for you.

he exits.

Zach	We need to go to a motel too.

Harry has changed into a suit, stands at a urinal.

Harry   Pardon me.

Leonard   I don't have time.

Harry   Leonard Kildare?

Leonard   Yeah.

Harry   Well, I'm just a fan.

Leonard   You were there?

Harry   The First Meeting of the Renegade GD Shareholder Faction in this very motel.

Leonard   I thought it was invite-only.

Harry   The kinds of things that were said there need to be said. For far too long Man has dwelt in sin. A voice in the wilderness cries You Prepare to make the way of the Lord.

Leonard   I'm not a very religious man. But I noticed a lot of you renegade shareholders are.

Harry   Parties within the ownership of GD Confectionery and its sister organizations in the conglomerate are with us. They conducted high-end surveillance of the Hunting Trip and staff meetings & know all about the current direction of the Company. We have converged on this motel because we are looking for leadership. The Shareholders will speak with a unified voice. We've outlined a strategy by which the Board will be convinced the Shareholders wish to kill the power of the current CEO and Director of Marketing, promote you to CEO and Director of Marketing/New Products.

Leonard	How do I know this isn't a test of loyalty?
Harry	It is. A test of your loyalty to traditional values. There's more of us than there are of them. That's our big advantage. And we're all Christians! Read the Bible. It's revolutionary!! We'll be contacting you again.

Harry disappears.

SCENE EIGHTEEN – SECURITY UPDATE

Calculatrice rushes into CEO's office.

Calculatrice	Fitz, I just got a report from security. There's a rumor a tiny renegade faction of shareholders is spreading misinformation about the Shitballs prototype. Can we assume it's just a pocket of the reactionary and the short-sighted?
CEO	Rumors don't just go away. They grow until they're true. How can we kill this?
Calculatrice	I think you know.
CEO	Ignorance is so dangerous.
Calculatrice	What's dangerous is executives without loyalty. What's dangerous is the rumor this band wants us hanging from the beech tree in front of the pond with the fountain. Have I brought this on?
CEO	Sometimes I look at you, I feel like my head's been taken off and put back on.
Calculatrice	What?
CEO	Sorry.
Calculatrice	Capitalism is made of death threats. You've got to listen

CEO	I do.
Calculatrice	Don't look at me that way. You're not ready to make the kill.
CEO	I remember the first time I saw you.
Calculatrice	A fine horse to bet on.
CEO	Only natural.
Calculatrice	Your generation and class. The clipper class. Cutty Sark.
CEO	Construction workers look at you.
Calculatrice	Differently. You have the power to act on the relationship you set up between your eye and the subject of your gaze.
CEO	That's power.
Calculatrice	That's worth guarding.
CEO	I know what I have to do.
Calculatrice	You'll fire him.
CEO	Yes.

she pulls open his desk drawer, to reveal a .45 magnum.

Calculatrice	The right tool for the right job.

CEO exits. Calc goes to the phone. Dials on speaker. Across stage, Michael checks his pager. Daniel enters from elsewhere.

Calculatrice	Daniel, I don't know why you show up at all the wrong times.
Daniel	I'm still on the listserv.

Calculatrice	But that stuff is confidential department security.
Daniel	When you have total access, you leave parameters behind if you ever want to get back in.
Calculatrice	What do you make of the leaks?
Daniel	Leonard doesn't have the balls to lead a shareholder rebellion against Fitz.
Calculatrice	It is Leonard.
Daniel	I thought that was common knowledge. What codes are you using?
Calculatrice	I'm concerned for my safety. Do you still pack?
Daniel	This is suddenly getting way too much like my new office. You know were going public. NASDAQ. It's all very dog and pony. Underwriters everywhere. You've got to learn to sift through the noise.
Calculatrice	You'll make a killing.
Daniel	But I've decided to jump when the stock hits. I want to do something I believe in again.
Calculatrice	Then lend me your Glock.
Daniel	Can't do it. I've got a lot of shit to sift through in my own office. I gotta watch my back. At least until I can jump ship.
Calculatrice	What happened to that loyalty? It's all just a pile of shit to sift through to you, what's the new job really all about?
Daniel	The challenge of it. I guess. If you can't believe in the product, what motivates you is just letting yourself go, get completely wrapped around the work itself. And that's enough. You hope. Acrobatics without a net.
Calculatrice	I'M GETTING MY ASS KICKED HERE.

Daniel	Anything I can consult on?
Calculatrice	Non-D.
Daniel	non-disclosure to me?
Calculatrice	I don't have another minute.
Daniel	You should have said. I'll get out of your hair.

Exit Daniel, crossing near Michael. Michael is approaching the office but hides his face to shuffle by Daniel.

Michael	That was Daniel McDonagh. You know Daniel McDonagh?
Calculatrice	You know his work?
Michael	Sure, those the interviews in Brandweek?
Calculatrice	Why do you read Brandweek?
Michael	Well, I'm with a group. Interested in how public opinion is created.

Calculatrice pulls a book out of her desk. In the same place a gun was in CEO's

Calculatrice	Is the name of that group the Maoist Progressive Party? You never said you were a member of the Maoist Progressive Party.
Michael	I'm a supporter of the Maoist Progressive Party.
Calculatrice	Oh come on, don't you trust me?
Michael	It's not my role.
Calculatrice	We're running out of time. I stayed up all night last night, reading the Party Program. "First thing we do, we take out the ad agencies." How can you be drawing the picture of a revolution that puts the ad agencies on the block first, yet, you study Marketing and Corporate

	Motivation?
Michael	I've got a security update for you. A renegade faction of the shareholders is burning you in effigy. They don't like the course the Company is taking.
Calculatrice	There have been death threats on our voice mails.
Michael	Don't tell just anyone what you read at night.
Calculatrice	Fitz is a good man.
Michael	He's CEO. He will burn you for it. He has to please the majority of the shareholders. If the reactionaries become a majority in time he will sacrifice you in a second.
Calculatrice	There have been death threats on both of our lives. Fitz and I have a class interest.
Michael	As executives?
Calculatrice	We're our own class now. No one will stand with us. What can you do.

beat. He places a pistol on the desk.

Michael	You know how to use one of these.

She picks it up. Checks it.

Calculatrice	It's not loaded.
Michael	It's not loaded but there's a tradition that you don't point a gun at someone unless you're going to use it.
Calculatrice	OH COME ON. I'm not going to shoot you.
Michael	If you really want to defend yourself, you have to be prepared to go all the way. OK? this is it, two to the chest and one the the head. When you're ready to go two to the chest and one to the head, without compunction, you're ready to load and carry.

Calculatrice	Where's the safety?
Michael	Ok we know it's not loaded. But you're pointing it at me. There are rules in handguns.
Calculatrice	Fuck the rules.
Michael	Someone's going to get hurt.
Calculatrice	That's what guns are for. Where have you been. Doesn't the Maoist Progressive Party train out in the desert?
Michael	Of course not. We teach that the revolution is something you prepare for. That you don't strike until the iron is hot.
Calculatrice	Bullshit. That book doesn't teach that. It draws the picture, it chooses targets and it names names. Like I am a target, for Leonard and his forces.

beat.

Calculatrice	I'd like to offer you a position in Human Resources. Salary. Benefits. 401K. Interested?
Michael	Philosophy has to be alive. It can't be like a hermit crab. It would be an honor.
Calculatrice	Are you now or have you ever been a member of the Maoist Progressive Party? And how do you get in?
Michael	Well, it's not easy. But I could give you something to read.

SCENE NINETEEN – MORNING AGAIN IN AMERICA

Harry and Leonard addressing a small crowd.

Harry	In the course of human events, it sometimes becomes

necessary to break with the leadership of a certain organization. And although we have only been able to gather a representative handful of the shareholders here today, I believe this is the start of a revolution in this company that will set us back on the course we know is to the mutual benefit of all. I give you the next CEO of GD Confectionery, Mr. Leonard Kildare.

piped in prerecorded massive applause and cheers.

Leonard I'm here today to represent a new tomorrow for GD Confectionery. A return home. Our hearts are at rest in what is most familiar, the values we were all raised with. Mom. Big cars. Three squares a day. And more, much more. A fair deal. A solid handshake. Knowing the market. The ability to know the market and meet it in the field. A level playing field. Not one dominated by feel-good management jargon, spacey music and "affirmative action" hiring quotas. It's time for us to take back the reins. At GD Confectionery, night has fallen for too long. The company has been run by tiny people with their little ideas. But with Kildare and the Renegade Shareholders Association, it's morning again at GD Confectionery.

Harry I'd like to ask the Future CEO what Jesus would have done in this instance?

Leonard Jesus. Well, maybe not everyone sees it this way, but Jesus came to kick a little butt. Jesus said get out there into the trenches. The people want to do what's right, but they can't, there's a homosexual agenda in the schools, femi-nazis in the media, liberals in office legislating reverse racism, OK? Reverse Racism. The Law. OK? Discipline, hard work, achievement. Whatever happened to a country driven towards a black bottom line? We're in the red, because too many people think there's something wrong with turning a profit. Get over it. We need a return to a strong dollar, strong leadership behind strong U.S. corporations. Blueblood. The Founding Fathers would agree, and you know, I think God the Father would agree. I think that's why it has In God We Trust on the money.

CEO   Let's be solution-oriented.

Leonard   Well, the situation is problem-centered.

Calculatrice   And obviously the solution is going to have to be principle-centered.

Leonard   But not on your principles, Missy.

Calculatrice   Missy? Missy?

CEO   I just want to confront the rumors, Leonard.

Leonard   I'm accountable. Ask me anything.

CEO   There's been a lot of loose talk of takeover. The stock price has been fluctuating like a sound wave...I think its in our mutual interests that we come to an agreement. Calculatrice, help me out here.

Calculatrice   We're battening down the hatches until we can reestablish stability.

CEO   We're placing you on administrative leave, but we're not firing you. That would look bad. So we're going to request and require you to not leave the compound until the stock price stabilizes.

Leonard   This is unconstitutional. You have no jurisdiction. I question your authority.

CEO   I am the Chief Executive Officer of this company. Executive means one who executes, policy or sentences. Think of me as your government.

Calculatrice   Government is force.

Leonard   This is completely illegitimate.

CEO   We thought you might think so. This is a second per-
                formance counseling statement. Please sign it.

Fitz pulls back his suit jacket to one side, with one arm.

CEO   This is a .45 magnum. You're on administrative leave.

Zach   Delivery!

Calculatrice   Is it?

Zach   It is!

Calculatrice   Shitballs?

Zach   Straight from the plant!

Calculatrice whips over to the box. Rips it open.

Calculatrice   It's the physicalization of a dream. Look at the color in
                the packaging.

Leonard   Merry Christmas, OK? This is also a .45 magnum. The
                tree of liberty is occasionally fed with blood.

CEO   Calculatrice! Hit the floor. We're going live.

They both cock.

CEO   It's really stupid it has to come to this.

Leonard   This is the land of the free. You've lost touch with the
                constituency.

CEO   You've never represented a majority of the shareholders,
                just the skimmed scum of the top of the pond. Surface
                reaction, bile in a stomach, not food. Not nourishment.

Leonard   I represent right and wrong. I am the unforgiving angel.
                You want to defuse the current impasse?

CEO   Of course.

Leonard	Return all shipments of Shitballs to the plant. Have the plant incinerate them.
CEO	I can't do that. We've invested in the product.
Leonard	God dammit, Fitz! Is THIS for the new technology? Is THIS our new brand? All THIS for MARKETING? Is this worth dying for?
CEO	Yes.
Calculatrice	Leonard, it's not just developing a market, it's creating something new.
Leonard	You're sick.

Leonard shoots the CEO in the head.

Leonard	Oh my god. oh my God. Did I actually just DO that? Oh my god. Is he dead? Is he going to die?

Leonard has lowered his piece. Calculatrice stares incredulous, and then, a bit late, pulls on him. He looks up.

Calculatrice	Leonard Kildare. You're fired.

beat

Leonard	What are YOU going to do?
Calculatrice	I'm. Thinking.
Leonard	I feel awful.

He leaves.

Michael   Candy-makers. Union of confectioners, I address you directly in the rank and file, since your union leadership won't return my phone calls. As the representative of the new Human Resources Department, I'd like to deliver an update from the provisional executive staff. CEO Fitz Hirshhorn has been fired. The leadership of the company is in crisis. If we don't get the support of labor, we collapse.

Sheryl   Management doesn't give a shit about our opinions.

Michael   In the past, yes, this corporation has never had the leadership to know how to express interest. Until now.

Tenisha   This'll be good.

Michael   10 People run this company 3600 work in the plants and offices. The power we have is huge. They never tap it. I know about you all. They don't talk to you, right, until its time to renew your contract.

Tenisha   Then its like we want to borrow money.

Michael   You can't just let the bosses have all the power. You union will sell you out unless you get into it, take a stand for your interests. The Board is going to elect a new CEO.

Sheryl   What I heard is the Board is gonna give it to Leonard Kildare, right?

Michael   They're thinking about him.

Sheryl   I ain't got nothin bad to say about the man who signs my check you know what I'm sayin? I Ain't gonna say nothing about him. But she might.

Tenisha   Well last Spring he intimidated the union with threats of outsourcing...the economy's good. But every time the Union tries and get us a piece he's like Mexico Mexico.

Sheryl	Because he believes in the United States of America.
Michael	What is America?
Sheryl	I don't know. I mean, you know. I'm pissed off I'm even here.
Tenisha	It's a machine.
Michael	Leonard Kildare - is he one of us? Is he the best of us?
Sheryl	He's the best of what we've got. He loves America.
Tenisha	He hates his body. You see him driving, or touring the plant, he's stiff.
Michael	Exactly. Hates it.
Sheryl	What's the choice?
Michael	The Board is calling an emergency meeting for tomorrow at dawn. If this union ever meant a thing to anyone then this union needs to lead, for once. 'Cause this corporation needs leadership. It has to come from here. There is one qualified to lead. Her name is Calculatrice. She's not perfect. But out of everyone in management, she's the one who can defend our interests from that greed weasel, Leonard Kildare.
Tenisha	You don't remember. She used to be down the kitchens.
Sheryl	I remember her pretty good. Is she real? You all love her. Love, love, love. We don't trust no one in management. What do we really we know about her? It's been a while since she was working down in the kitchens.
Michael	Questions like those that will lead us out of this crisis. Being from the union, she can make this a truly democratic company, where wages can rise, people are free to develop new skills.
Tenisha	Well, where do you think she got the idea for Shitballs?

Michael	From you?
Tenisha	Everyone likes comedy. I told her to use what she had. She didn't always used to believe in herself.
Michael	I know some unions real well some I don't know so well. This one, I don't know so well. I need you to spread the word. Have everyone in the kitchens put the pressure on the shop stewards. It's Calculatrice, or it's death. Businesses aren't democracies. Get the Union to put pressure on the Board to elect her CEO or prepare to defend your lives against a hostile swine. He hates Unions. He hates gays, women, blacks and vegetarians. He hates cat-people, vinyl collectors, he hates labor organizers.
Sheryl	You mean Communists?
Michael	That's a whole other ball of wax.

SCENE TWENTY TWO – THE POSITION IN SALES

FBI	Calculatrice?
Calculatrice	Yes?
FBI	We've really got to talk.
Calculatrice	Please. You must be here for the position in sales.
FBI	Ben Karadza, FBI.
Calculatrice	Tell me about yourself, Ben.
FBI	I care deeply about Truth and Justice, and America.
Calculatrice	Good start. You know we're mission-driven company. I appreciate that.

FBI	I'm here to ask you....
Calculatrice	Let me continue to drive this interview, Ben, but I appreciate your initiative. How important is the product to you in your motivational mentality?
FBI	I don't quite understand the question.
Calculatrice	If you began selling for us, how important would be believing in the brand, and the usefulness, the taste and the quality of the GD Product?
FBI	Look, I used to sell. I'm more into research now, with the organization I'm currently with. But I know from selling that the product doesn't matter one bit. It's my self-esteem that drives my pitch. It's me believing in myself. They said, "You're tall. You're a natural".
Calculatrice	Umm. So, the values of the brand per se don't inspire you to....
FBI	Well, let me rephrase that. It's the self-esteem question first, then the product that's important to my process.
Calculatrice	So the brand and the product are important. Actually the second most important factor to your success.
FBI	But I don't want it to seem like I'm flip-flopping.
Calculatrice	You are flip-flopping.
FBI	Well, I just don't want to seem like I'm making excuses.
Calculatrice	It's obvious you know how weak excuses always sound, yet you don't know how to stop making them.
FBI	I'm not.
Calculatrice	You weren't?
FBI	I'm already employed.

Calculatrice	You mentioned that, and we have an intelligence division of our own. It's called sales. I consider them our finest vanguard. They are armed with the principles of the company. We supply them with the highly crafted, full-color printed matter. No expenses are spared. They are on the front lines, direct to the merchants. And you're going to come in here with your little ego and your concealed recording devices, taping the proceedings without my consent, in the name of a bloated Federal bureaucracy meddling in the affairs of a candy company that just wants to do something really good?
FBI	I just wanted to ask you a few questions about the seriousness of your this political marketing campaign. I wanted to say you're not playing the kind of game we can play. You didn't hear it from me, but my bosses are not going to support you if Leonard Kildare mounts a counter offensive.
Calculatrice	I'm sorry, Ben. We only have a limited amount of time for each candidate. Like my old business mentor used to say, "Always walk your guest to the door."
FBI	I could save you. I could renounce everything.
Calculatrice	Don't damage the first impression.
FBI	I think I'm in love with you.

she sits back down.

Calculatrice	Then serve the people. You want to serve me, serve the people. Give up everything you have, sacrifice your reputation and your weapons. Drop it. And start work for us in Sales.

beat.

FBI	I can't do it.

beat.

Calculatrice   Thanks for coming down today.

Calculatrice at the Union meeting. Everyone is present.

Calculatrice   Fellow Candy-Makers. Can I be frank? The rich have run
                    this country all its life. You see their control in union-
                    bashing, downsizing, bad tv, lousy products. They want
                    us to be slaves to stupidity. But they are the slaves, to
                    what they call "the Good Life."

                    I've stopped production today. Because we are going to
                    be attacked. If anyone wants to leave, you may. But I'd
                    like to ask that you hear me out.

                    The rich sell us nothing but mediocrity, despair, depres-
                    sion. Their religions say this is the way it will always be,
                    and should be. They seem to believe in hell on earth for
                    us. They want us locked into being the byproduct of the
                    machine. But I'm here to blow apart a secret. To their
                    own the rich teach a special formula: Their God is the
                    belief that one has control. You are proactive, you can
                    divine, you have a choice. You've not the sum of what
                    has happened to you, all your actions don't have to be
                    reactions. Break your habits. They are not special.
                    Freedom has been the exclusive domain of the rich, the
                    rulers, the parasites, the managers. Until now.

                    Boom bust and crush. How much of this do they expect
                    us to tolerate? How many depressions and recessions?
                    If Leonard Kildare had gotten elected to the position I
                    now hold, your wages would stagnate while the para-
                    sites and the economy thrived.

                    I speak with you today, here in the majority, the people
                    who don't always want more of everything. The people
                    who instead just want to survive, and be happy, and take
                    care of each other. I thank the union that brought me
                    into this company for the opportunity to address you

here today.

The structure of GD Confectionery has undergone certain changes. Let's push it, until it flips. There is a quality of freedom apart from the fake freedom of the rich. Freedom is not judged by the ability to make a killing in your lifetime. Freedom doesn't mean taking your position in the dog-eat-dog feeding frenzy. It means changing your mind. Breaking with the things breaking us. Take control over your own life first, then we take the whole machine.

Labor has only one control: we have our hands on the levers of production. We can shut down the whole thing at any time. It's time now to draw a line in the sand, look up, and say NO. The way you demagogues do things is not as perfect as you think. You're fired. You say you have the vision of excellence, that you are elevated by your sense of quality? I don't think you act like it. We'll show you excellence. We'll show you a work ethic.

But how do you jump start history when it has slowed down?

Force. The midwife of every society pregnant with the new. Leonard Kildare and friends don't want you to vote for me as CEO today. They will most likely mount an armed attack on our new structure. With the white horses of their cocaine-funded intelligence organizations. We will build something stronger than that to defend this factory. We have freedom. We have real democracy. I say we take a stand. Who's in? Who's down for the whole thing?

SCENE TWENTY-FOUR – LAST CALL AT LUCKY'S

Michael and Calculatrice. Back at the Union Bar. Lights up slowly on Michael as the same Magazine song plays. Enter Calculatrice.

Michael   Have a drink.

beat.

Michael   It's important to relax sometimes at night.

Calculatrice   I told you. Taking a break from drinking. There's no time. Didn't you see that email. Where have you been?

beat

Calculatrice   Bartender. Soda and bitters.

Michael   Hit me again.

Calculatrice   Michael.

Michael lets out a long slow sigh.

Security at the plant has to be airtight. Another time, we might have time. What's the romance of two individuals compared with what we've created together, all of us, my ideas, and us working with a fighting union.

Michael   You could have called me back.

Calculatrice   What happened between us was fun. But I'm not going to marry you.

Michael   You're laughing at me. You should be saving me. I think I can give everything to the struggle. But I'm somehow losing steam. I think I want to protect you. I can't explain it.

Calculatrice   I like the fierce respect we all have for each other on the factory floor, have you felt it?

Michael   I knew it was there all along.

Calculatrice   I didn't. I was in that union and I didn't. So I got into marketing, when they wanted to pull me in I let them. I wanted it.

Michael   But where do you want to win? In the free market or in a real revolution?

Calculatrice	The free market is a myth.
Michael	So then?
Calculatrice	I'm running things here with all the intensity of the greedy system that trained me. Because we have more. We have love. It's the kind of power that makes us unde-featable. You and Zach continue to drill the workers with all the intensity of a straight army. Because we have more. We will never be defeated because our forces are transformed by the spirit of this revolutionary love.
Michael	I'm frightened. I think there are two streams inside you. Your training as a worker and your training as an executive.
Calculatrice	I was born in a donut shop. I was raised serving cops. I starting grinding my teeth at age 13. C'mon let's go home.

enter Harry.

Harry	"Woe to those who demand strong drink as soon as they rise in the morning, and linger into the night while wine inflames them! ...what the Lord does, they regard not the work of his hands they see not. Therefore the nether world enlarges its throat and opens its maw without limit."
Michael	Harry, where the hell have you been?
Harry	Hitchhiking.
Michael	I thought you turned on us.
Harry	I thought they knew God. I'm not perfect. I decided in the middle of betraying you that I was back on your side so I was just infiltrating them. I just want to do what's right. Will you forgive me?

beat.

Calculatrice	Harry has an intelligence briefing for you.
Harry	Leonard has gotten the support of the police and FBI. There's a good chance he and the renegade shareholders and raid the factory and offices tomorrow. They are well-armed.
Michael	Oh god.
Calculatrice	What do you mean 'oh god.' This is called working.
Michael	Mao said only fight the battles you know you can win.
Calculatrice	We can win this one. We have something they don't. We're gonna win this one tomorrow and set a track record. Last call.

SCENE TWENTY-FIVE – FINALE

Calculatrice, Michael, Zach, Harry, Union members all behind a barricade of desks, with hunting rifles and AKs and M16s. The sounds and shells and assault weapon fire surrounds them. Enter Sheryl leading Daniel, bound.

Calculatrice	Daniel, how the hell did you get in here?
Daniel	I still have a working code.
Sheryl	We found him at level three.
Daniel	Can I get these cuffs off?
Sheryl	In time.
Calculatrice	I can't believe your code is still fresh.
Daniel	Maybe I was meant to be here. It never expires. I thought I might need to get back in someday.

sound of explosion and alarms and shouting.

Calculatrice   Get behind the barricade. They're shelling that side.

he does.

Daniel   The CEO of Coke is dead.

beat.

Calculatrice   I'm sorry to hear that.

Daniel   Lung cancer. He was good. Drank a lot of Coke, smoked a lot, polyps at age fifty-seven, but still. His successor is the one who once appeared before a board meeting with a live garden hose and said, "What do you do when your competition is drowning? You stick a live hose in his mouth!"

Calculatrice   Too bad our competition isn't drowning.

Daniel   I saw them on the way in. They were helping the police shut down the roads. There's a growing civilian protest at the roadblock, things are getting a little tense. Could get ugly. How many workers are in the factory here?

Calculatrice   Thirty-six hundred.

Daniel   And how many of them are in the Union?

Calculatrice   All of them.

Daniel   So how many are defending the compound?

Calculatrice   I'd say we have about thirty two hundred uninjured right now. The rest are either casualties or doing publicity work in the area.

Daniel   You mean marketing?

Calculatrice   Fuck marketing. You've come home and you don't know the place.

Daniel	What about the power of the powerbrand?
Calculatrice	What does Coke do? It dissolves the baby teeth of children. What does Shitballs do? It destroys the nerves of people like Leonard Kildare. Get in here.
Daniel	The CEO of Coke never took off his jacket. All the executives on his floor followed suit. The air conditioning was always up ten more degrees. Can you imagine the esprit de corps of that office?
Calculatrice	That esprit de corps is nothing but fear. Look at ours. It breathes fire. You always said the U.S. needed a revolution, but that people weren't ready. I've got thirty two hundred workers defending our organization from Kildare, his forces and his friends in the security apparatus. The CEO of Coke is dead. I'm sorry, because I know you always admired his discipline. But it's like I always said, you gotta believe in the product. Now, do you know how to load a Kalashnikof?
Daniel	No.

she unlocks his hand cuffs.

Calculatrice	You know nothing. Get out of here the way you came.

CURTAIN.

SEALOVE, MANAGER

Act I

Sealove mowing the lawn, singing as if for an engine that is not listening.

Sealove:

DEATH!...to the Grass

DIRT!...under blades!

SWIPE!...Electric cuts!

This is what I know.

This is me doing a good job.

I am older now

I change the bag when it needs changing.

I don't leave clumps of grass.

Don't mark my laziness with a trail.

This is me, older

Sealove, manager

DEATH!

And if not death, at least a close trim!

DUST!

Atomized grass on the back of my neck

GRASS!

Healthy super fertile lawn of their pride

LIFE!

Long and itchy, smelly and wet.

Lights up on joe joe, in a backwards baseball cap, in the house, upstage, playing bass with large sweeping dissonant intervals.

There is a boy called hope because he is

Not a mower

Glad his older brother has moved back in

And taken over

The sticky mowing,

He has never slipped his hand

Under the mower

Been later asked

What were you thinking?

Never felt the short thick cut of life and fear and

DEATH!

And if not death, at least a close trim!

DUST!

Atomized grass on the back of my neck

GRASS!

Healthy super fertile lawn of their pride, of my pride

LIFE!

Long and itchy, smelly and wet.

Sealove looks up at joe joe, keeps singing and mowing:

What are your skills?

Can you manage?

Have you killed?

Hiring and firing

With an iron will?

Have you applied

To be a CIA assasin?

Have you misplaced your passions?

DEATH?

Don't you believe it. It was just a close trim.

DIRT?

It's under everything.

Even my old wall street corner office.

GRASS?

And then a little coke?

Yes, yes, yes

 If you're buying.

LIFE?

Hiring and firing.

Starting and stopping again.

Sealove stops the mower and the music thus also stops. Joe joe stops playing .

Hey loony boy called hope

Playing bass like me in my old room

Come on down, here

Pick up a rake

Even now i can still get lazy

He takes off the bag from the mower. Joe Joe comes downstairs.

Sealove   You didn't think I could still be lazy. You thought I was
                 too old to get lazy. So did I. But what do you know. I
                 suddenly feel lazy.

Joe Joe   Dork. Of course.

Joe Joe Enters, with a skateboard.

Sealove   What?

Joe Joe   You said you never did coke.

Sealove	I'm not straight anymore. I told you that. You get older, you try everything.
Joe Joe	You get fat, happy and disgusting.
Sealove	You get tough.
Joe Joe	And you know what's in your fat.
Sealove	If I was starving, I'd have something to burn.
Joe Joe	POT you Pot belly yuppie. DisGUSTING. Oh no, it's a natural high. It's brain poison. Can you remember my name?
Sealove	Joe Joe
Joe Joe	Look at you. fat shiny as a plastic beer beach ball. Something outta the Quick Stop out at Seven Oaks.
Sealove	good place to skate, right?
Joe Joe	You won't see me buying anything.
Sealove	But you profit from the plastic stuff sold there, just being there, you profit off the asphalt. You love Quick Stop. You love that kind of architecture, skating around the commerce of the beach balls and the beer.
Joe Joe	skating a little yeah!
Sealove	Imagine the managers there. They're working with a profit and loss statement. You call it your P&L. You manage with the P&L. You get it every month, you can see. It get's pretty tight. Even if you used to skate, suddenly you don't really need skaters skateboarding in the parking lot without buying anything. The older, paying people don't like it, you're adding a hassle, hassle is loss.
Joe Joe	Go back up north, old man
Sealove	This is where I was born

Joe Joe	Take a shower
Sealove	I am mowing the lawn
Joe Joe	You mowed the lawn yesterday.
Sealove	I'm mowing the lawn, and I like to be sure I'm doing a good job. It is definitely under control. The lawn is my responsibility, now.

beat

What's your responsibility?

Joe Joe	I work at the Snack Bar. When I take a five minute break, I swim. When it's this hot. You're bugging me with the sound of the mower, every day.
Sealove	Joe Joe! Look, it's Sealove, Manager. The greatest manager of our time. The manager with the philosophy to make it happen. Sealove, your brother has returned home, for the summer, maybe forever. Don't you see the potential here?
Joe Joe	You used to live here?

Sealove stops.

Sealove	Of course. I'm your brother.
Joe Joe	When? I don't remember.
Sealove	You were nine.
Joe Joe	If I can't really remember, how am I supposed to talk about this?

beat

Sealove	I'll be done soon. You wanna go to the comic book store after?

beat

Joe Joe   I'll think about it.

SCENE TWO

Early in the morning the next day. Mom is dressing Sealove for mass. They are in Sealove's old room. Joe Joe is dressed already, sitting up on his loft bed. Mom is picking out horrid, old stuff from Sealove's old closet. Sealove is trying things on .

Mom   Have you been drinking enough fluids?

Sealove   Yes

Mom   The radio said it was 96 yesterday.

beat

Mom   Try this one. Your godmother got you this, remember?

Sealove   Really? No.

Sealove ties the tie.

Mom stands back, takes him in, clothes-wise, doesn't like it.

Mom   It clashes with the pants

Sealove   Yeah

Mom takes the tie off, adjusts the collar. She goes to the closet.

Sealove   What mass are we shooting for?

Mom   The 8:30. I always think the church is cooler, earlier
                 on in the day.

Sealove   Cooler?

Mom	Not as muggy
Sealove	It's air conditioned
Mom	Still.

She comes back from the closet with yellow yuppie dotted suspenders and matching bow tie.

Mom	Try this on. You always looked smart in this.

He begins tying the tie. She looks at him, split focus, in a mirror.

Mom	Did I tell you Phil Sherry is in his third year of law school down at UVA? And just loving it?
Sealove	Of course.
Mom	Says he's no longer interested in going into politics, though.
Sealove	Sure
Mom	No really, he has changed. You'd really like him now.
Sealove	So he went to charm school....
Mom	Listen, he's going to be going places and he's an old friend of yours.
Sealove	He was a friend of mine in fourth grade. I knew I hated him by the sixth.
Mom	I didn't care for him around then too.
Sealove	And all throughout high school.
Mom	But he's changed now.
Sealove	So have I.

She looks up.

Mom	We're going to be late for mass.
Sealove	Then let's hurry up.

She brings him his blazer.

Mom	I hope in all of your New York life you were still trying to make sense of it all.
Sealove	Definitely.
Mom	Remaining open.
Sealove	Always.
Mom	Searching. I pray every night you will rediscover your faith.
Sealove	It wasn't faith, it was belief.
Mom	Of course. But you have to have faith.
Sealove	I have faith.
Mom	You said you don't believe in God.
Sealove	I... Well I don't believe in...this. Where we're going...
Mom	Then why do you come along?
Sealove	You said I couldn't live at home unless I came to mass every week.
Mom	I don't just want you to come along for the ride. The Lord doesn't need your hollow prayers. I want you to have your life together. Our souls are not at rest until they rest in you O Lord.

He sings, he goes to her:

Sealove	Death! and if not Death, at least a close trim! Have you applied to be a CIA assasin? Have you misplaced

your passions?

Mom   Sometimes I wonder what's gotten into you. I mean, what's gotten inside you, do you hear what I'm saying? What happened to the Christian values you were raised with? What has taken control over your soul?

Sealove   My mind. I am a manager.

Mom   There's room for everybody in the house of the lord. Socialists, Managers, "New Waves," everybody.

Beat

Sealove   We're going to be late. I don't consider myself on time unless I'm five minutes early.

SCENE THREE – MASS

Sealove, Joe Joe, and Mom enter the church to processional music :

Chorus:

KICK ASS.

GOD IS KICK ASS

WHEN YOU SAY GOD

I SAY KICK ASS!

KICK ASS.

GOD IS KICK ASS

WHEN YOU SAY GOD

I SAY KICK ASS!

Mom's solo:

He is money to the poor and needy

He is peace of mind to the rich

Some boys of this world are too good to believe

It must be the sexual itch.

Sealove:

Some say there is no God

Some say he's just a old trend

But when you say God, Think of your Kick-Ass Dad!

Your Kick-Ass Dad never bends!

Everyone!

KICK ASS.

GOD IS KICK ASS

WHEN YOU SAY GOD

I SAY KICK ASS!

Father Bob and Joe Joe as altar boy come up the center aisle.

Father Bob:

Imagine him coming in glory

Imagine the people that are wrong

Imagine those people down in the dark pit!

We'll still be singing this song:

everyone:

KICK ASS.

GOD IS KICK ASS

WHEN YOU SAY GOD

I SAY KICK ASS!

KICK ASS.

GOD IS KICK ASS

WHEN YOU SAY GOD

I SAY KICK ASS!

Music ends. Father Bob addresses the mass of all gathered.

Fr. Bob	Peace be with you.
Mass	And also with you
Fr. Bob	Boy are we in for it today.
Mass	We are?
Fr. Bob	The humidity, I mean.
Mass	We'll be inside.
Fr. Bob	Watching the game?
Mass	Of course
Fr. Bob	Well that's a good starting point for my sermon today.

He adjusts his posture.

Imagine a bookie that knew the outcome of every game.

Wouldn't you want to place your bets with this bookie?

Don't you think you could sort of see it in his eyes

when you were trying to beat an impossible spread?

And I do mean impossible. Imagine him.

This is a bookie who knows the outcome.

He decides the outcome, the winners, the losers.

He decides who is kick ass, and my friends, who is not.

Mass	AMEN.
Father Bob	My friends, this bookie is our God. He is the Father.

He has a Son who is also the Father.

And He is also the Spirit who is also the Father, as well as the Son.

And He is the book maker. He is the word.

We can say nothing without the word.

I can not speak but for the book maker touching my lips.

Mass	AMEN.
Father Bob	So boy are we in for it today. Stay inside, I tell you
	It's gonna be a scorcher.
	But if you do go outside, at half time, go with God.
Mass	AMEN.

Music. Joe Joe and Mom present the chalice and bread up the center aisle. Father Bob takes the gifts to the altar. Begins the consecration, everyone is silent.

Fr. Bob	Just like Jesus, we are unsure. Just like Jesus, we live in a world of strange powers. We can pick up the sword or we can break bread. Jesus broke bread, and breaking the bread said, take this, all of you, and eat it. This is my body, to be given up for you. Not to be given up to you, this is my body to be given over to Rome and the soldiers. To be given back to you when Rome is done scourging and injecting it.
Mass	Blessed be God forever
Fr. Bob	This is the cup. Cup of ever-lasting life. Should we drink from this cup? I don't know. Jesus said we can either drink from the cup or we can put it down. You can pass it, it's up to you. But if you drink from it, believe this: living forever means God knows everything you do. If you're in heaven, this isn't bad. But If you are damned, well, you might wish you had not drunk from the cup of

everlasting life. I don't want to tell you what to do but...Fruit of the vine and work of human hands it will become for us our spiritual drink.

Mass   Blessed be God forever.

Fr. Bob   This is the body and blood of the most high, Jesus Christ. What do you know?

Mass   Lord I am not worthy to receive you, but only say the word, and I shall be healed.

Everyone lines up to receive. Father B holds up a wafer, says "Body of Christ," and each says "Amen." First the Chorus Leader, then the Chorus. The Chorus goes back and plays an instrumental, passionate version of the verses of God Is Kick Ass.

Sealove and Mom go up last , he is hesitant as they approach up the center aisle. Suddenly he stops.

Sealove   I am a manager.

Mom   You got fired

Sealove   I don't believe in God.

Mom   It's not you do or you don't. You need to, that's pretty clear.

Father Bob   Either way. You can never really be free from doubt. And it's not essential that you are. Body of Christ.

Sealove   I want to imagine myself on death row, walking down the last hallway, about to be executed, like Christ was executed. This is my body, convicted, and about to be executed.

Joe Joe   This is my body, soft as a lamb but not as innocent.

Mom   This is my body. All I want to do is something good.

Joe Joe   You're a virgin if you don't have sex with somebody else

	Are you a virgin if you have sex with yourself?
	Seven times seven I've had my lucky, virginal self
	This is my body, soft as a lamb unsure of itself
Sealove	Did I really believe that was the body of Christ?
	I did I remember it now, white in my eyes
	Now what does that say about my will to believe
	This is my body and mind: employable, easy.
Father Bob	Body of Christ a truth all alone
	Executed yes, but spirit enthroned
	In the world that ignored him, that forsook its own
	This is my body, salvation gunned down by Rome
Sealove	I want to believe but I know I can not
	And I want to receive just like I was taught
	Its true I was fired, but when you get hired
	You'll say you believe anything, whether or not.
Father Bob	Body of Christ.
Sealove	Amen.

He receives.

SCENE FOUR

Joe Joe and Sealove outside the church.

Joe Joe   Watch this.

Hip Hop beat. Joe Joe tries to really kick it:

GOD is a pod

in space waiting for me

the cool side of the pillow

when I fall asleep

He is the fabric

once it is cleaned

the feel of the cotton

the smell of the bleach

Sealove:

God is a dream

You choose to believe

You believe in dreams

out of a need

I did too

we've had the same dream

Blank spot there now

the color of bleach

Joe Joe:

I love the smell of the bleach

like the smell of a beach

orange and fresh

my first memories?

God is a pod

in space waiting for me

The cool side of the pillow

When I fall asleep

And if not God what?

what crawled up your butt?

God never hurt you

the door ain't shut.

Sealove:

Am I a fool for thinking I'm free?

Will I be broken for choosing my dreams?

God was a Pod in space waiting for me

But I've gotten picky and prickly about what I believe.

Joe Joe:

Who do you talk to as you fall asleep?

the soft fabric?

the smell of the bleach?

God is a rod

to swipe at the teeth

the milkweed pod

floating in the breeze

Sealove:

Those things are things

no character to cheat.

Joe Joe:

Character?

Sealove:

You personify things

Can't you see anything

not in the context of you...?

Joe Joe:

But what makes me me?

                     In line for communion you chose to receive

Sealove:

It felt right somehow, to suspend disbelief

Joe Joe:

But did you really receive him, did you really believe?

Sealove:

I remember well I used to believe

Joe Joe:

Who are you?

What have you seen?

I am what seems true in the best of my dreams.

A sense warmer than feel

Realer than Real

I dream, I scream

of a Thing without seams

God is a pod in space waiting for me

The cool side of the pillow when I fall asleep

He is a ship

and though I may trip

someday I'll return, he'll recognize me.

Mom parks the car and exits.

SCENE FIVE

Joe Joe gets ready to go to work.

Sealove   The smell of bleach and sugar cereals. America.
                 What's for brunch?

Joe Joe   Dorkola, I gotta go to work.

Sealove:

Who's your manager?

They probably

trained under me.

What's the name of your manager?

They started us at two an hour

What are they paying now?

Joe:

I don't want to know anything

I just gotta go to work soon

I don't want to work in the Snack Bar

I don't want to start to know how to work

Sealove:

You've gotta know all you can

The more you know, the more you make

If you don't want to know

You yourself will be nothing to know.

Joe Joe:

I have a couple of managers

Plus some I don't know their names

How should I know if they remember you?

I don't remember when you lived here last

Sealove:

I want to know you

I want you to remember me

I want you to know who I am

I am not from here, although I lived here

Ten summers ago

I built a ramp

and I skated late at night out under the lamps.

You were four, you were bored

You were as fun as a houseplant

But you watched me from upstairs

Falling from my first ramp.

Joe Joe:

My brother Sealove was a skate-punk

But now he's 'a manager', head full of junk

But you're not my boss, and I'm just your bro'

We both live here now, That's all I know

Sealove:

You admit a lot there,

But Puppy Child, there is more

maybe, I can show you.

Call in sick to the Snack Bar

Joe:

I don't want to know anything

Nobody calls me "Puppy Child" anymore

I don't want to work in the Snack Bar

I don't want to start to know how to work

Sealove:

we...we could go for a ride

Do you want to go for a bit of a drive?

we...we could go for a ride

Do you want to go for a bit of a drive

Joe:

As long as we stop,

at the comic book shop

Anything worth knowing,

is in the ink drops

In the non-adult section

of the comic book shop

Everything worth knowing,

worth making the stop.

Both:

In the non-adult section

of the comic book shop

Everything worth knowing,

worth making the stop.

The music of this exchange builds as lights fade.

SCENE SIX – THE CREEK.

Enter Sealove, Joe trailing, reading the X-Men.

Sealove   I remember when that place was just baseball cards
                     and coins.

Joe   You're talking like an old fat guy again.

Sealove   Well I once bought this rusty old coin thing there, I mean
                     it looked like it was uh...a bottlecap caked up with all
                     this corrosion. They said it was from Ancient Egypt. I
                     said "How Can You Be Sure?" The guy said, "Because it's
                     my business to know these things."

Joe Joe   Uh huh

Sealove   I bought it. I took it home, taped it down into my book.
                     With a ball point pen, I wrote next to it, Ancient Egypt.

Joe   Shouldn't you be like, reading the Help Wanted section,
                     back at home?

Sealove   This place is important. Even more than the comic
                     book shop, if you'll believe me.

Joe   I've been here a million times

Sealove   But have you ever been this far up?

Joe   Up the creek? Up shit creek?

Sealove   This is not shit creek.

Joe   Drink some of it then.

beat.

Sealove   Dmitri and I used to follow the creek for miles. In sum-
                     mer and even in winter. Winter was easier sometimes,
                     it would freeze over.

Joe	Well, it doesn't freeze anymore.
Sealove	In summer sometimes there were these black snakes in the trees.
Joe Joe	What are we doing?
Sealove	We are exploring uncharted territory. I want to show you something.
Joe	If you know what it is, it's not really uncharted territory.
Sealove	Pretend this is all a movie. You'll feel better.
Joe	What kind of movie?
Sealove	Your kind. What kind is your kind.
Joe	Japanese Animation. I can't believe they were out of stock. Nobody cares about what I like.
Sealove	All right. Let's pretend we're 200 years into the future.
Joe	Watch this. Woof-woof. I am the last of the dog people. There was a nuclear war a long time ago, but everything healed. Except the fascist bastard fishheads have taken over the water supply and the dog people live in the desert. And we are looking for the lost river. But this is the lost river. But it's poisoned.
Sealove	We have to find the source. That's what Dmitri and I were always looking for. The spring it springs from. Or the sewer pipe.
Joe	We have to find the source, because it's the only thing unpoisoned. The fascist bastard fishheads make Dog Boy make money. But he doesn't want to make money. Because it hurts. But it's the only way for him now to get unpoisoned water from them.
Sealove	What happens the next time the fishheads make him make money?

Joe	It is sad. But it will be a big scene and he will rat the dog people out. He will tell the fishheads where to find them in the desert. He is weak, but he just wants love.
Sealove	He can't rat!
Joe	I don't know. He can't find the fountain source. Everything he drinks is poisoned. Everything is meat and sugar and he can't find the fountain source.
Sealove	His brother Sealove will show it to him.
Joe	You don't know where it is. You never said you found it.
Sealove	I am a manager. I found it in a different city. Far from this one. Fascist bastard fishhead central. I will show you where to find it.
Joe	You better.
Sealove	OK, this is it, this is step one. I think this is the same bend in the creek. This is the scene of the Dmitri Fire.

Mom pops up from behind a bush.

Mom	It's illegal to light fires in a public park.
Joe Joe	This is a park now?
Sealove	Guess so. IT'S OKAY WE'RE DOING THIS FOR A MERIT BADGE.

Mom pops back down again.

Joe	Why a fire?
Sealove	Dmitri fell in. I told you we used to walk up it, a lot in winter, when it was frozen? Almost frozen. We were curious about certain spots along the edges that became unfrozen and then froze again. Beautiful textures. Dmitri stepped on them and on one, went in up to his thigh. Some kids were playing hockey nearby and they

laughed hard at us. So we limped away and built a fire. No one had ever built a fire around here before, there was plenty of good kindling under the snow. We made this fire huge. PYRO JOE, we used to call each other. It was a fun fire. And I remember how scared we were when...

Mom   YOU CAN'T BUILD FIRES IN A PUBLIC PARK.

Sealove   Right, that lady called to us from the nature path. She really scared us. Oh no, we're going to get reported. We are breaking the law.

Joe   I don't want a record.

Sealove   In this moment, then, we have to become the law. If you don't want trouble, you have to impersonate people who are right. We have been boy scouts together for a little while, so we'll yell back, IT'S OKAY WE'RE DOING THIS FOR A MERIT BADGE.

Mom *(out)*   Oh well, if they are boy scouts, they obviously know what they are doing. Uniformed agents of our nation's values obviously have the right to usurp the park authority.

Sealove   That's right baby, so like they say in the scouts,

Joe   "Don't Fuck with the Fire."

Mom disappears again. Sealove sits by the creek bank, catches his breath, makes a transition.

Sealove   Why did we come out here every chance we got?

Joe   You wanted to find the lost tribe of the dog people.

Sealove   Instead we found older kids playing hockey, who laughed at us when we fell in. 'We told you not to step on the ice there.'

Joe   Fish heads.

Sealove   Dog people don't have to hide at the creek. They won't be around fishheads forever.

Joe   I know.

Sealove   Fires are a load of fun.

Joe   You can cook shit too.

Sealove yawns, lays back for a nap. Joe Joe pulls his cap over his eyes and does the same. Enter Klein, addressing Sealove.

Klein   Sealove, I'm really looking for two things out of you. That you develop a management protocol and that you train the workers with it.

Sealove gets up off the ground. Puts on a clip-on tie.

Sealove   Yes.

Klein   This office is a mess

Sealove   Yes

Klein   Somebody needs to clean it up

Sealove   Def...

Klein   And I mean a deep clean.

Sealove   And what's the best method of doing that?

Klein   You tell me.

beat.

Sealove   Ok, well first...

A loud beep comes from the intercom.

Klein   YEAH!

Intercom   Mrs. Schwarzkopf from International Wrap Factory on two.

Klein	OKAY. *he turns to the intercom* Hi. Absolutely. Absolutely. I don't know. Absolutely. Thanks. B'Bye.

hangs up. Looks around desk. Hunches over more.

Klein	Where were we?
Sealove	The best method of implementing a new management protocol
Klein	Yes
Sealove	Well there's a lot here that needs changing. First things first, the language...

intercom beeps.

Klein	Yeah?
Intercom	Giorgio from 'She Goes To Your Head.'
Klein	Aaaaaa...Take a message, I'm in a meeting.

Click.

Sealove	Thank you. I think people here have a tendency to try and do everything themselves, not work together. I think they fear one another.
Klein	Really?
Sealove	Not enough trust.
Klein	A ha?
Sealove	By the way, if I could interrupt, I haven't gotten my tax forms yet.
Klein	You haven't been hired yet.

Sealove	But I've been working here for two weeks
Klein	This is just you training period.
Sealove	Oh.
Klein	Anything else?

Intercom beeps, louder.

Klein	Yeah?

Sealove gets up and grabs a phone. He picks it up, listens, holds it to his chest. He speaks to Joe Joe who has gotten up, put on a clip-on tie and slumped into another office chair on casters.

Sealove	I've got a client here says he was promised service three weeks ago and still hasn't received it.
Joe Joe	Have him call the network
Sealove	He did. They told him to call here.
Joe Joe	Does he have his merchant number?
Sealove	Yeah.
Joe Joe	Did he reboot his system?
Sealove	Yeah, Yeah.
Joe Joe	It's out of my hands.
Sealove	What is?
Joe Joe	You're wasting your time to talking to him anymore. Hang up the phone.
Sealove	I'm not going to hang up the phone on the guy...
Joe Joe	We've done all we can do.

Sealove	This guy is out there on the front lines of retail and we have to support him!
Joe Joe	It's out of my control. The network should take care of him.
Sealove	Is that the procedure?
Joe Joe	It's just what we do here.

Exit Joe Joe

Sealove:

I'm high up the creek

Klein:

You're way downtown

Sealove:

I'm doing a good job

Klein:

You're just screwing around

Sealove:

I've just been hired for the job

Klein:

You just called me a fat slob

Sealove:

I am looking for the source

Klein:

You are dreaming, of course

Sealove:

Feels just like a humid afternoon's end

Is that the sound of a rushing stream

Both:

Or the fax machine jamming again?

Sealove:

I am proactive, I'm on the go

Have a lot to contribute to the firm I know

Klein:

I like you a lot, that's why it's hard

To say I'm sorry but we're letting you go.

Sealove

Feels just like a humid

afternoon's end

Is that the sound of a rushing stream

Both:

Or the fax machine jamming again?

Joe Joe:

This is your vision of being a man

Jobs and bars and marketing plans

Your dulled edge helps you ease into it.

But I am straight and don't have to believe it!

Sealove:

I am with you, the one who gave you

Your first straight edge tape

I am back here, it's still up here

It just takes a different shape.

Joe Joe:

Look at them! You salute them

You're in their decay

They can't look me in the eye

You're getting older in the same way

You used to be hard

and set against this

waltzing with the swine...

Sealove:

Joe Joe try and understand

I can be hard and I can be soft at the same time.

I can be hard and I can be soft at the same time.

I can be hard and I can be soft

ALL:

Feels just like a humid

afternoon's end

Is that the sound of a rushing stream

Or the fax machine jamming again?

Joe Joe and Sealove are sitting where they were before their nap. No music save for the sound of the creek. Sealove jerks awake.

Sealove	But I'm the manager with the philosophy to make it happen!
Joe Joe	What?
Sealove	I can be hard and I can be soft.
Joe Joe	You say the word philosophy an awful lot

Sealove takes a deep breath.

Sealove   The creek sounds nice, doesn't it?

Joe Joe   Better than kids whining for ice cream.

Sealove   At the snack bar?

Joe Joe   Kids never worked a day in their life.

Sealove   Little fucks.

They get up, brush off, laughing. They walk back to the house. Lights fade.

Act II

The lawn has gotten long and unruly. Sealove sits in front of the house drinking the last two cans of a six pack of Red Dog. He is bloated from the beer and the humidity.

Joe Joe enters with a box of stolen ice creams from the Snack Bar.

Joe Joe:

White latex dripped on fake gold

"We're not building a Swiss watch."

We built a world out of particle board but

"We're not building a Swiss watch."

Warped grade-C lumber is cost effective!

"We're not building a Swiss watch."

Sell ice cream when tots scream, dog-boys work hard!

Punch the clock like a Swiss watch.

Sealove:

You are a real boy. You have a job.

Joe Joe:

"We're not building a Swiss watch."

Sealove:

Did you steal these ice creams? Tell me the truth.

Joe Joe:

"We're not building a Swiss watch."

Joe Joe:

Whatever happened to wanting to know?

Sealove:

"We're not building a Swiss watch."

Joe Joe:

Whatever happened to a lawn to mow?

Sealove:

"We're not building a Swiss watch."

Sealove:

It's not easy to do things well

Joe Joe:

"We're not building a Swiss watch."

Sealove:

You get tired. You get beat down.

Joe Joe:

"We're not building a Swiss watch."

Joe Joe:

I am NOT one of you

You can't see my dog paws under my hands

I am going to the creek

I am going to make a swing.

Sealove   Out of what?

Joe Joe   Out of rope.

Sealove   Good luck

Joe Joe   You're not helping.

Sealove   The trees leaning over the creek

               always fall in the creek.

               Your swing tree's gonna make a nice bridge

               in a couple weeks.

Joe Joe   Good bye.

Enter Mom from behind Sealove, exiting from house. She watches Joe head down to the creek. She looks at the yard.

Mom   If someone doesn't cut the grass soon, there are

	going to be complaints. The neighbors are going to think there's something wrong with us.
Sealove	I'll explain everything.
Mom	Has Joe Joe said when he was planning on cutting it?
Sealove	A dog doesn't cut the grass.
Mom	I don't think that's very funny.
Sealove	It wasn't supposed to be funny. It was supposed to be true.
Mom	Your brother is not a dog. I didn't give birth to a dog.
Sealove	I don't think you did. He says he's a dog, not me.
Mom	Have you been talking to him?
Sealove	Yes
Mom	Where did he get this idea?
Sealove	Maybe he had it himself.

beat.

Mom	Do you think it was those comic books?
Sealove	Yes. No.
Mom	Will you find out?
Sealove	I'm trying to mom, I'm trying. It's hard. I'm in a transition.

He makes an "I'm in a transition" gesture.

beat.

Mom *(tenderly)*	Take it seriously.

beat.

Sealove	I'm going to the store. I'm taking the car. Is that ok?
Mom	How many beers have you had?
Sealove	One
Mom	And the one you're holding?
Sealove	Is another one.
Mom	Well, a walk will do you good. When you get back we need to have a serious talk.

Music. Sealove moves to edge of stage but hears this:

Mom:

My two boys.

They scare me so much.

They can be touched

Only with noise

What are they?

A dog and ex-manager?

Is this the new branch here

Of the family?

Permanent decline

And the grass grows thick

They don't care a lick

For this heart of mine

But my boys

God tell them what's right

Push them towards light

Free them from noise

Permanent decline

And the grass grows thick

They don't care a lick

For this heart of mine

But my boys

God tell them what's right

Help them fight the good fight

Free them from noise

Sealove in Quick Stop store, outside the Seven Oaks mall. With a six-pack of Red Dog.

Clerk	Do you have ID?
Sealove	Yes but not on me.
Clerk	I need to see ID.
Sealove	I bought beer here two days ago. You sold it to me.
Clerk	They're cracking down.
Sealove	Look, there are two ways to run this, with the letter of the law, or with the spirit of the law. You know I'm old enough to buy this, so you won't be breaking the spirit of the law, the essence.
Clerk	I'll get fired.
Sealove	Come on, you won't get fired if you figure out how to do the best job possible here.
Clerk	You're not the Mystery Shopper, are you?
Sealove	Look, this is not a test. I just want to show you a tool. This is called Reason Over Rules Self-management. The best job possible is something no one can tell you how to do. You gotta figure it out.
Clerk	How do I figure it out?
Sealove	By using your head! What's your philosophy of customer service?
Clerk	Philosophy?
Sealove	What is it that keeps you going?

Clerk	Five twenty-five an hour.
Sealove	But if you had to say why this job wasn't so bad, what would you say?
Clerk	I don't know. You see a lot of people...
Sealove	Exactly! The People!
Clerk	Everyone wants something from the store.
Sealove	Right, and therefore, your job here is about...
Clerk	Getting people what they need.
Sealove	And what do I need?
Clerk	A six pack of beer.
Sealove	And why am I buying it from you?
Clerk	Because maybe I understand that you need it.
Sealove	And even though I don't have ID now...
Clerk	You're willing to sign a piece of paper saying you're old enough and give me three bucks extra for the hassle.
Sealove	Now hold on there, my friend...
Clerk	"Only I know how to do the best job possible here."
Sealove	I really don't have the three bucks extra though.
Clerk	Well, then you don't have to sign the paper neither.

Takes beer back.

Little beat.

Sealove	Nice talking to you.

Clerk   Nice talking to YOU.

SCENE THREE

Outside the store.

Gary   Excuse me

Sealove   Yeah

Gary   I really liked the way you handled yourself back there.

Sealove starts to laugh, then stops when he sees Gary isn't laughing

Sealove   Well, thanks...Yeah, I used to be a manager.

Gary   Retail?

Sealove   Mostly, yeah.

Gary   I'm expanding my company, and would really like to
                   talk to you about opportunities.

Sealove   Oh, OK.

Gary   Can we sit down sometime?

Sealove   Sure, How about now?

Gary   That would be great.

SCENE FOUR

Back at the house. Mom is yelling up the stairs at Joe Joe. He is in his room.

Mom   Joe Joe, could you come down here please? Joe Joe?

He enters.

Mom   What are you doing in there?

Joe   Nothing

Mom   Nothing? Why's your door always closed?

Joe   Ayooof.

Mom   There's nothing you can't tell me. We are a family, we confide in each other. I'm worried about you and your brother... Has he ever talked to you about sex? Is that what this dog acting thing is all about?

Joe   Has he ever...?

Mom   Is that what it is?

Joe   I just like to act like a dog sometimes.

Mom   Okay. But has he ever talked to you about sex?

Joe   Sex? Um. um. no. Except.

Mom   Except what?

Joe   Once, he said one thing.

Mom   You can tell me anything. I'm your mother.

Joe   Once, on vacation.

Mom   On vacation?

Joe   When I had just turned thirteen. He said now you're thirteen, you will start feeling things. And that you might start doing things to yourself in your bed, at night, when you are alone.

| Mom | Uh huh. |

| Joe | And that he used to...that he started to...um...well, when he was 13.... He said he wished someone had told him about it. So that he wouldn't feel guilty about it. |

| Mom | And what did he say this was called. |

beat.

Joe *(nervous laughter)* I can't say it.

| Mom | Say it. |

| Joe | Mom. |

| Mom | Say it. |

| Joe | Awwyyoof. |

| Mom | MASTURBATION. MASTURBATION? |

| Joe | I'm going back upstairs. |

| Mom | You are going to get out there and mow the lawn. You are NEVER going back upstairs. You are NEVER going back upstairs. |

SCENE FIVE

Gary and Sealove enter a diner. They sit down, the scene resumes twenty minutes into their conversation in a restaurant.

| Gary | Imagine - when you play your computer at chess, the machine never makes a wrong move. You can't hope it wont see something. To beat it you play a cleaner, sharper game. In life, you can't count on emotions when |

it comes to economics. Nobody gives anything away, nor should they even want to. To win, you have to get smart, play the game, and beat the machine with its own rules. By being better than the machine.

Sealove	People will always act in their own interests. Marx said so himself. That's neither good nor bad, it's just a fact.
Gary	Are you a Marxist?
Sealove	I'm a Post-Marxist.
Gary	We can go there later.

beat.

Sealove	Everyone thinks they are the one exception to the rule, everyone places their bets on a slim chance. They're playing the lottery.
Gary	Exactly. Economics isn't "cruel." It's the truest understanding of the material world.
Sealove	Yeah!
Gary	You're familiar with the philosophies of Werner Erhardt?
Sealove	No
Gary	But you've heard of est. The Landmark Forum?
Sealove	Um...No
Gary	Everything changed in my life when I read the story of Werner Erhardt. Would you have thought that a used car salesman leaving his wife and kids in the Mid West would go on to become the greatest mind of our time?
Sealove	Um...no.
Gary	Nor would I. And Yet! Well, this is it, in a nutshell, these are the principles: Most relationships just do not work.

Why? People live in the past. People are always playing their memories onto each other, like they are film projectors, instead of moving on, into the present. Being with that person, now. Which leads to the second principle: people don't change. The only way to make relationships work, is to first ACCEPT people as they are.

Sealove   Hmm. Like, my old friend from 4th grade, Phil Sherry. Super competitive at football by always bringing up obscure NFL rules. Years later, he's graduating Law School, my mom want me to schmooze him for my future. And we BOTH know he's a weasel. But SHE wants me to think that he's CHANGED.

Gary   She probably wants to see you become effective.

Sealove   I am effective.

Gary   Where's your beer?

Sealove   This world. Is fundamentally devoid of justice.

Gary   Be specific for me.

Sealove   Jesus, Specifics are everywhere. Mumia Abu-Jamal. The growing chasm between rich and poor.

Gary   Again, be specific for me.

Sealove   How about the specific way you get your ass kicked by banks when you're poor? Suddenly your level of customer service goes from mediocre to lethal. And I know what good customer...

Gary   Yes, but also understand banks have an oblig...

Sealove   My mom. OK OK take my mom. I've had the same song in my head since I was a teenager, when we first started to fight. And this summer, moving back, I finally started to write that song down. But I can't sing it for her. It's too honest.

Gary   Your point

Sealove	Where's the justice here? No! I'm finally beginning to get it. I understand this world's justice now: honesty is for losers. If you're honest, you get shut down. You don't get to finish your song. And people don't change.
Gary	Do you love her?
Sealove	I can't fight it. I was always like AAAIIIIIEEEEYARRGHAAAA. Spit on love. Whatever. But Yeah. Yeah I do.
Gary	Does she love you?
Sealove	She always says so.
Gary	OK, does she accept you? Has she permitted you to be?
Sealove	"Permitted" me?
Gary	Are you a Marxist?
Sealove	Probably. I mean, I'm a Post-Marxist.
Gary	Does she permit you, as a Post-Marxist, whatever that terms means, all the things that term means to you.
Sealove	Um...No.

beat.

Gary	Then she doesn't really love you.
	I'm sorry. Most relationships just do not work. It's time to repair the world.

beat.

Sealove	What does your company do?
Gary	There are certain things everyone needs, right? Toilet paper, deodorant, phones. What if you get ten people together to get the stuff wholesale from the suppliers?

Sealove	Because retail supports a network of middle men.
Gary	But why should we pay those mark-ups? The suppliers just want their wholesale price, they don't care who they're selling to.
Sealove	Sure.
Gary	Are you with me so far?
Sealove	Of course.
Gary	You look skeptical.
Sealove	Not everyone needs toilet paper, deodorant and phones.
Gary	There will always be a radical fringe, but we're talking about most of the people, most of the time. Now, those initial people, that initial group has a good thing going with these suppliers, let's say. What they're going to want to do is get their friends in on the deal. OK?
Sealove	Um, ok.
Gary	Let's say each person in the original ten person group can get ten friends in on the wholesale deal. Now for the advantage of getting in on the deal, the friends of the original group pay a little extra to the original group member that got them in. They don't get exactly the same low price, but they're still getting a deal. And this way, the original group members are getting a great deal, plus a little what's called...what?
Sealove	Residuals
Gary	Residual income, right. Just like a conventional sales force. "Ledger income." Totally legitimate, totally legal, you incorporate, you see.
Sealove	What do you call yourself
Gary	Four Star Distribution

Sealove	And the original group?
Gary	That was just a story.
Sealove	But what did the original organization call itself?
Gary	You mean?
Sealove	Who is this.
Gary	AmWay.

beat.

Sealove	Geez...why does that name give me the heebie jee-bies?
Gary	I don't really quite know, but it's like that for a lot of people...Which is why we don't say it at first.
Sealove	Still, I wish you had.
Gary	Well, I'm sorry.
Sealove	I'm looking for a job.
Gary	This is a job, if you decide it is. You just have to decide.
Sealove	See, I used to be a Marxist. No, I mean, I think I still am. But the free market seems to be so dominant, and In the push and shove of the natural forces of the market, I saw two kinds of roles open to me with my unmarketable liberal arts degree. I could become a Salesman, or I could become a Manager. Being a manager was harder, because you had to deal with people. The same people day after day. But being a salesman seemed to be all about image, you know being overwhelmingly, brightly handsome. The Teeth. So, without really having to choose, I was a manager. More improvisation. Content over form, you know...a more philosophical approach.

Gary	You'd be a great salesman.
Sealove	Thanks. If I give you five dollars, would you buy me a six pack of beer?
Gary	I think you're old enough to buy your own beer.
Sealove	I am, I just don't have my ID here. It's back at the house.
Gary	Can't you go back and get it?
Sealove	I could. I don't want to cause, I don't want to, right? What's your name?
Gary	Gary
Sealove	Gary, can't you get this for me, please?
Gary	I don't drink
Sealove	You don't have to drink any of it
Gary	Well, I don't support drinking either. I thought you were a manager.
Sealove	I am a manager. I'm in a transition.
Gary	And you're looking for work.
Sealove	Yes, real work. Something I can believe in.
Gary	Good luck.

He exits.

Sealove and mom in the kitchen.

Mom	Joe Joe says you met someone last night who offered you a job.
Sealove	Yeah.
Mom	I think it's about time you found something if you're going to stay.
Sealove	But this guy was an agent.
Mom	An angel? What?
Sealove	Yes! An angel of death! Deep cover. Career track. Global security assasin.
Mom	A what? An assasin?
Sealove	He wouldn't say. They never do. They can't. But I think he was "State Department."
Mom	Phil Sherry was talking about becoming a diplomat. It's a highly respected profession. Keep that in mind.
Sealove	But everything this guy said was worthless.
Mom	Well, we only hear what we want to hear sometimes, right?
Sealove	I know what I heard. I just talked to him to prove to myself that I don't want his kind of life. I will never be a diplomat like that. I will be diplomatic in the things that I do, but I won't wear those masks. Underneath is death.
Mom	Would you tell me, what is so wrong with being a diplomat? What is this big message you have for the world?

We always showed you a lot of love.

Sealove   I accept that

Mom   Somehow, it was never good enough.

Sealove   No, it was good. Love? Yes, okay I accept that. More
                 than just that, Mom, I accept you. I decided last night, I
                 have to stop trying to change you.

Mom   Thank You.

Sealove   Not that I could, I mean that's just it. But it's important
                 that I recognize this, see? I get free when I stop trying,
                 when I say, "I Openly, wholly, totally accept you for what
                 you are." Now, I'd like to ask for the same in return.

Mom   If you think I'm going to condone some of the behav-
                 ior, some of the immoral...sick....

Sealove   I'm not going there. I'm talking about who I am, not what
                 I've done. How about you meet me halfway? Could we
                 just agree that accepting each other is something we
                 both need to work on?

Mom   There's nothing wrong with me. I have never had to be
                 in therapy. If you're saying there's something wrong with
                 me, you are dead wrong, mister.

Sealove   Mom, just give me a minute. Just be quiet for a sec-
                 ond, let's...

Mom   You will never understand the way I love you. A child is
                 a mother's heart walking outside her body. Sealove, you
                 will never understand how I love you.

Sealove sings his fucking heart out:

You are the suburbs

I am the city

You remain here

Because you do not permit me.

Love?

Love is easy

Tag. we are related.

I am queasy

I need you to say you know me

Before you love me

You say you love me

I need you to say you accept me

Before you love me...

If you want to fly

Gonna have to open your eyes

Suck me in

Like a new smoke you've never tried

You flinch but I say

Savor this, understand

Sweeter than the smell of sand

The sugar on my hands

What were the names

Of the faces I have loved?

Ask me how she was

Versus how he was

What were the differences to the tongue?

Love me

We're all adults here, in

DC

The gleaming city

You want me white

Like the scrubbed history

But I am leaving

Back up North

To the tiny island, in the river

Where I am allowed to be me

Suburbs of DC

You say that you love me

You can say what you want

I was taught it's all diplomacy

I've got 25 bucks

I can get on that bus

You want to bomb New York City

You want to bomb what permits me

Here

I am just the past

I am nothing but the things i've done

I am your memories of my sins

I am not even your son

But the things that I did, I did cause I had to

Or really wanted to and could

I didn't do them just to break with you

But I need to

I need to

Leave leave leave

Love love love

"I love you, you love me"

We're a loving family

A love as soft as

The hands around my neck

Who Do You Love?

You love me as a baby

Someone who didn't do these things

And that's okay

I'll be your baby

As long as you can let me be me

Too

I am Two!

SCENE SEVEN

Father Bob, Mom, Sealove and Joe Joe sitting around the kitchen table. There is stand off silence for a number of beats.

Mom   SO.

beat.

Sealove   Yes.

Mom   Does anyone have the solution?

Sealove   Joe Joe?

Joe Joe   What?

Sealove   What's the solution?

Joe Joe   I don't know anything.

Mom   Now, Joey, you can't say that, you've had a good edu-
                cation, at good Catholic Schools, right, Father?

F. Bob   Immanuel Kant said, "All we can know is that we know
                nothing."

Sealove   But that's so useless!

Joe Joe   It's true. All the things I know already I don't want to
                know them anymore either.

Mom   You're job is to go to school in a couple weeks, and
                learn all you can.

Joe Joe   woof.

Mom   You Are Not A Dog.

Fr. Bob   Mary, I don't think Joe Joe really thinks he's a dog do
                you Joe Joe?

Joe Joe	woof woof.
Sealove	Try Spanish.
Fat. Bob	Esta....Esta tu es uno...uno lupo?
Mom	Joe Joe Doesn't speak Spanish.

to Sealove.

Mom	Listen mister, it's either add or subtract. Your brother is in a crisis.
Sealove	I know. I was in the same one nine years ago.
Mom	And look how you turned out.
Sealove	Exactly. My point exactly.
Fr. Bob	Now, Mary, I don't think Sealove turned out badly.
Sealove	I'm a complete atheist. I believe in things wholeheartedly and then they disappear. Jobs, loves, ideals, disappear. Perhaps if I hadn't believed so hard when I was here, when I was young, when I was a believer.
Fr. Bob	You were president of the Youth Group...
Mom (*to S*).	Is that MY fault? Did I fail so badly as a mother? Tell me, where did I go wrong?

beat.

Joe Joe	arf.
Mom (*to Joe Joe*)	Spit it out!

(*to Father Bob*)

Do you see what I mean? Do you see why I say we Need what I Say we need?

Fr. Bob	Perhaps we could try prayer. Does your family ever pray the rosary?
Sealove	Only in the car on long trips. I like it then, actually. It helps to pass the time.
Mom	I was wondering why you said it with us then.
Sealove	And you were thinking, "Well, as long as he is saying the words..."
Mom	Do you think I'm stupid? Do you like...
Fr. Bob	WHY don't we say the rosary? It can't hurt. We can go around the circle, trading off being the leader. It's not about hierarchy.
Mom	I'll start. OK. Our Father, who art in Heaven, hallowed be thy name, thy kingdom come, thy will be done, on earth as it is in Heaven.
ALL	Give us this day our daily bread and forgive us our trespasses as we forgive those who trespass against us, and lead us not into temptation, but deliver us from all evil.

Sealove *a little louder, sort of to everyone*

> What a run-on sentence!

Mom, Bob & Sealove	O most blessed virgin, never was it known that anyone who prayed to you, or fled to your protection was left without recourse. Despise not our petitions.
Sealove	Of course she's going to Despise Our Petitions, our petitions are selfish!
Sealove	Hail Mary, full of grace, the lord is with thee, blessed art thou among women, and blessed is the fruit of thy womb, Jesus.

Everyone responds in English, except Joe Joe who speaks the words in woofs.

All	Holy Mary, Mother of God, pray for us sinners now and at the hour of death...
Sealove	Hail Mary, full of grace, the lord is with thee, blessed art thou among women, and blessed is the fruit of thy womb, Jesus.
All	Holy Mary, Mother of God, pray for us sinners now and at the hour of death...
Sealove	*Staged whisper to Joe Joe at a volume the elders can not pretend to ignore.* What a funny prayer, we seem to be going inside her body, and then we decide we are going to die.
Mom	Okay, that is it. I am convinced it is you. You are at the root of the problem.
Sealove	I am saying the prayers!
Mom	You need to say Only the prayers!
Fr. Bob	The False Prophet is he who acts like a man of god.
Mom	He knows all the words to all the psalms, because he is a trickster.
Fr. Bob	But in the end, all his promises are hollow.
Sealove	Isn't there room for a critique? You know, for improvement of the language?
Fr. Bob	These prayers have been around for thousands of years. Do you think the Son of God needs a lesson in grammar from some middle-class smart aleck down on his luck?
Sealove	Yes.
Fr. Bob	You're wrong, mister. You are dead wrong. You have a lot of work to do, A LOT of work to do. Before it's too late, I'd just stop and do some soul searching. What

happened to your spirituality? What are you replacing God with, yourself? You always were a leader in your community, whether it was the Youth Group or being a Manager. I'm sorry you got fired, but God didn't fire you.

Sealove   Jesus Christ.

Mom   Blessed be the name of the Lord.

Sealove   I really feel like a walk to the creek all of a sudden. Anyone else? I hope it's OK if I cut out a bit early here in the chain of prayers, but I hear Joe Joe built a new rope swing recently, and I've been dying to try it out. If you'll excuse me.

He exits. Joe Joe gets up, raises his paws, follows him out.

Father Bob looks at Mom.

Fr. Bob   You're right.

Mom   I knew it.

SCENE EIGHT

Sealove and Joe Joe back down at the creek.

Joe Joe   Have you ever had your heart broken?

Sealove   It's hard to say how many times.

Joe Joe   When was the worst?

Sealove   Probably when I lived here.

Joe Joe	Franca?
Sealove	I see her now. She was the spitting image of mom. But you grow up, you learn the limits of what you can't have. And why. You learn why for yourself. Some people have to find out the hard way. I did. She was paranoid the way all the adults here are, all the way back in high school, she was paranoid like she was 50. So grown-up. Her dad was an arms dealer, I think. They were all very pro-Contra. She kicked my ass at Model U.N. Last time I came down I saw her. She's still the same.
Joe Joe	State Department?
Sealove	World Bank.
Joe Joe	She was pretty.
Sealove	She hasn't changed. Pretty. And punitive.
Joe Joe	Have you ever broken somebody's heart?
beat	
Joe Joe	You don't have to answer.
Sealove	I'm not moving back in. This is our last walk to the creek for a while. Home is one big heartbreak. And yes, I think I broke a heart. Once. Not a woman. The only guy I was ever serious about became ambivalent and weird, he was older. I couldn't tell what he really wanted, or what I did. He wanted me to be serious, but was afraid of the word "commitment." It was all so goddam political. I left him for Sharon.
Joe Joe	I remember Sharon.
Sealove	The Christmas I first brought Sharon home, tough season. He kept coming into the store. With flowers. While all the customers were going crazy he would come in with a dozen roses and demand to talk to me. Finally he moved to Vancouver to go to medical school. I think he was the only heart I ever really broke. All the women I've

loved have been stronger than that. Stronger than me.

Sealove:

They say love

Who you are related to

It's arbitrary like a disease

Families

Say I love you

I love you, I love you

You better love me back, please

Let me seize

The reins of this humid day

And say

I know who you are

I love your quiet rage

As you're skating away

I love you for who are

There is a big difference

North and South, the big there and here

I gotta go back up North

Let me kiss you on the ears

Joe Joe:

I lie in bed

Pictures in my head

Red blood pumping in my heart

I want to love

I want to fuck

What if it turns out I'm too smart?

Love and it happening

Is so far away

I want to just forget about it for now

But in my blood is the pictures of dogs

Who want with a want that could bring down a cow

There's a big difference

North and South, the big there and here

You belong back up North

Where you can get kissed on the ears

Sealove:

I know it all

The smell of the Fall

And the pretty kids in white schools

All the kids act cool

And the cool kids rule

But you've learned to be smarter than cool

Joe Joe:

I'm not that smart

I have a dog's heart

Tell me how to change

Into something real

Sealove:

You want to shout about it

They won't talk about it

They stare at the ballgames

Out on the fields.

Both:

There's a big difference

North and South, the big there and here

You don't belong here.

Let me kiss you on the ears.

There's a big difference

North and South, the big there and here

You don't belong here.

Let me kiss you on the ears.

They hug and kiss. Sealove exits.

Father Bob, Mom, and Gary enter the creek hollow. they are wearing white sacra-mental robes. They seize Joe Joe and dress him in simple white garments. Blackout.

SCENE NINE

Back in church, in front of a font of water. As the lights come up, Joe Joe's head is removed dripping from the water by Gary and Mom. They hold him over the font. The garment is tied so that it restrains his arms. Father Bob stands in the center behind them, facing out with his psalter.

Father Bob:

Lord we stand before you with only one week of summer left.

Are we ready for this new season?

Prepare us to play the game as if it was our last.

To you we pray

They dunk Joe Joe

Gary & Mom:

Kick Ass! Hosanna in the Highest, Blessed be God Forever.

Father Bob:

When we are young we are sometimes too clever

You who knew us before we were born

You who know every smart-ass thing our siblings say

Before they influence us, and tie the mill stone around our necks

Clean our ears, purge our minds of things meant to be smarter than you.
                    To you we pray.

They dunk Joe Joe

Gary & Mom:

You are Kick Ass! Hosanna in the Highest, Blessed be God Forever.

Father Bob:

You are not shy and you do not pussy foot.

We love you because you are the upfront God

Anything Shy and introverted comes from the False One,

The Dark one, the two-faced trickster, the one who keeps secrets.

There are no secrets before you, and there is no shyness.

They dunk Joe Joe

All:

Burn it out of us, drown it out of us, as we drown it out of this one.

To you we pray.

You are Kick Ass, Hosanna in the Highest, Blessed be God Forever.

Father Bob:

You gave us dominion over the animals

You gave us language to name them

You who told Adam in the garden, call them what you like

Just don't forget what you named them for crying out loud

You are the Word, you are the language we use.

We are not dog-people, we are god-people

In the name of Jesus, who chased the false traders from the temple

In the name of the rage that fuels us against everything that is not you.

In the name of the fire that cleans.

Now.

Gary and Mom dunk Joe Joe.

O, Dogged False One

O, Sly Dark Shy One

I call you,

Leave the body of this boy, never to return

Get him ready for school in a week

Give him a sense of his duty to his mother,

and a knowledge of what's important in Life.

They bring Joe Joe up coughing and sputtering, water and mucus flies from his mouth and lungs. It even looks as if he has been exorcised, from all the shit he's coughing up. Suddenly, he barks.

CURTAIN.

RAPID CITY

SCENE ONE

Dawn in a desert in New Mexico.

Outside a garage, Sealove is sleeping on an old van seat, huddled against the desert night's cold. A bobcat, Zeusie, pops up from behind the van bench. She peers down at Sealove. She comes around and peers into his gaping mouth, observes him breathing. She slowly puts a paw over his mouth. Suddenly she holds it there firmly. Sealove chokes awake, as Lourdes comes around out from the garage. She is a fiftysomething highway mechanic. She walks with a slight limp.

Lourdes   Zeusie!

Zeusie scatters. Sealove sputters awake.

Lourdes   What, you 'think you're Mr. Touchy touch? C'mere. I'll give ya. Bag of mulch.

Sealove rubs his greasy hands into his eyes and tries to generate moisture in his parched mouth.

Sealove   I'm awake.

Lourdes has already turned away, and gone into the garage.

Sealove lights a cigarette.

Sealove   I dreamed a get away with it all after all kind of dream out here.

Lourdes comes back with a styrofoam cup of black coffee.

Lourdes   That was Zeusie.

Sealove looks at her.

Lourdes   I thought I would explain before this got out of hand.

Zeusie appears on top of the garage, wearing old welder-style safety goggles.

Lourdes   HEY! Where did you GET Those?

Zeusie dives back off the roof of the garage.

Sealove   This is before it gets out of hand?

Lourdes turns to go, but then stops and looks at the bike.

Lourdes   Jesus, daylight don't make it look easier.

Sealove   Last night, the fire was just a dream.

Lourdes   Still, it'll be fun right? Where's your tools?

Sealove   I slept funny. The fire was a horrible little big thing...

Lourdes   Where'd you say you were from again?

Sealove   New York

Lourdes   mmm. long way

Sealove   my bike

Lourdes   Caught fire.

Sealove   just over the border out of Texas

Lourdes   get used to it. Name's Lourdes.

Sealove   Sealove, nice to...

Sealove goes to shake her hand but she hands him a set of vise grips.

Lourdes   I know your kind. You think you have the take apart the
                 whole axle just to get the rear wheel off. You know the
                 bolts you tighten t' adjust the chain slack? Loosen 'em.
                 See what happens.

Lourdes turns to go, but Zeusie sneaks back in with a bouquet of sagegrass.
Lourdes notices gratefully.

Lourdes   Zeusie!

Zeusie stares at Lourdes with a cat's blasé disinterest.

Lourdes   C'mere pop op op giva mizz snuggles a wuggle!

Zeusie very slowly goes the other way.

Lourdes   She's gifted. But sometime's she's not too bright.
                 Know what I mean?

Sealove   sure.

Lourdes   Sure. Can I give you a word of advice? Don't be talking
                 about Texas.

Sealove smiles a little.

Sealove   Well

Lourdes   People round here will fucking hurt you.

Sealove   I can alway...

Lourdes   There's this Cop, by the name of Cody. Patrols the
                 whole county, and this county goes on forever. So he's
                 like a State Trooper and a local rolled into one. Owns the
                 hunnerd sixty acres near the exit 'fore this one. And
                 there's always someone Sniffin around on it.

Sealove   Texans?

Lourdes   You can smell 'em! Cody takes it personal.

Sealove   He sounds sensitive

Lourdes   You wish

Sealove   Hey, you got any cream? I got these patches of scabs
                 on my back....

Lourdes steps up close to him for a second.

Lourdes   You got big lips.

Sealove   I'm not protecting myself.

Zeusie walks by closely, walking in a deliberately "normal" human fashion. Lourdes begins to try to light a cigarette with a lighter that won't catch. She talks to Zeusie.

Lourdes   I know what you're doing. You're going up the truck stop, ripping off the machine.

To Sealove:

                 Plays poker, pays you in tickets, these tickets buy you anything they're selling right there. Bought me a carton of GPCs.

To Zeusie: You know you could hang around the shop more, help me do tires.

Zeusie stops and looks at Lourdes. Lourdes gives up with a quiet disgust.

Lourdes   Oh, allllll right. Go, get out of here.

Zeusie turns to go, but suddenly breaks out of the "normal person's" walk and sneaks away into a corner as Lourdes turns back to Sealove. Zeusie sneaks behind her, begins mocking the act of enjoying a cigarette.

Lourdes   I mention this because they have chapstick at the Truckstop.

Sealove   Oh, oh right.

Lourdes   Chapstick, bug spray, snickers, leeches, worms, frogs, you fish?

Zeusie jumps on her from behind, bear-hugs her neck, nibbles her.

Lourdes   Zeusie! If you bite me again I'm not talking to you again for a week!

Zeusie jumps off at once and runs off, behind the garage.

Lourdes   Ah hah! Knew that would do it. Get us some peace around here. She hates it when I don't talk to her. I ignore her instead of her ignorin me all the time. Becomes a test of the wills, and she forgets, my will is Fuckin' Steel.

Sealove   I better get started.

Sealove takes off the seat of the bike.

Lourdes   Ya see, I don't talk to her, she's never gonna learna talk at all. Who's gonna teach her out here? The fucking radio? I do not think SO! Round here, you don't learna speak, you don't get a good job. Good, yeah, get started. You wait any longer, yer gonna have a real burn. What size tire was that?

Sealove   18. Something 18.

Lourdes   Come again?

Sealove   18 hunderd or something I think...

Lourdes laughs

Lourdes   It's a '77? Gotta be a one-80 they don't MAKE 18 hunnerd

Sealove   Thanks

Lourdes   I'll go see what we got.

Lourdes disappears into the back of the shop. Sealove struggles with the rear axle, chain slack bolts, etc. Sealove has uneven abilities. Zeusie is stretched out on the roof of the garage, peering down, watching him. Lourdes shouts from within the garage.

Lourdes   So, how'd it start?

Sealove   Well. I love Texas. For some reason.

Lourdes   I Ain't heard a one.

Sealove   maybe those pieces it has jutting out of it. You keep going through at least pieces of it, you keep getting a taste of the old "Don't Fuck With Us."

In the window of the garage, Lourdes shoots a look, and then fakes a big yawn. Sealove tries out a Texas accent.

Sealove   "We have nothing to do with you, east coast number cruncher, ghost town of voice mail. We have bulls. We have oil."

Zeusie is getting down.

Lourdes   Texans come in here, like they own the joint.

Sealove   This is an idealization. Like a movie.

Lourdes   Yeah, right.

Sealove   Broad. People are friendly in a way to let you know they could snap you in half.

Lourdes   Texans come around here with Real Estate on the brain.

Sealove   as SOON as I crossed that borderline, out of Texas, I saw a ball of yellow white light fall from the bike. I mean, I just assumed I had a bag open. I assumed my rain pants were falling out.

Lourdes   I was in Texas once. To see the monument.

Sealove   Which monument?

Lourdes   I don't know.

Sealove   So I'm like, it's just another semi-important thing dropped and gone, I might go back and get it, I might do without it until I really need it and then I'll just feel way dysfunctional, right?

Lourdes   In my shop, we'd just say, "NON-Functional", as in, like, "he shore is actin' non-functional."

Zeusie has mounted the bike. She is acting like she is engulfed in flames, pretending to ride the motorcycle. Lourdes stands in front of the bike, arms crossed.

Sealove   No. The bike IS on fire. The ball of yellow white light is
                 fire, a wind, a curl, so dry just over the border out of
                 Texas, and the engine is either leaking oil, burning oil,
                 the pipes next to my canvas saddle bags, genius con-
                 traption, hotter than they ever should be...old bike, "air
                 cooled," right?

Zeusie turns to Sealove, hisses, bares her teeth. Turns back to motorcycle driving.
Sealove is struggling with the fire, as it spreads.

Sealove   The tire catches and crackles. The bag of clothes is
                 completely gone. The other bags are about to catch
                 but I whip out my blade, and cut them free, just like
                 this.

Sealove pulls out a switchblade and flicks it. Lourdes takes out her Eagle knife and
begins to clean her nails with it. Sealove acts like he's cutting the other bags.

Sealove   Just like this, Sacrificing my bunji cord collection.

Zeusie disappears again.

Lourdes   Bunji cords are cheap, just go to Family Dollar...

Sealove stares at the bike as it really is without Zeusie—charred.

Sealove   I kicked at the burning seat, I pounded on it and the
                 last pieces fell off.

Sealove is about to go kick the bike to demonstrate but Zeusie pounces on him from
behind. She wraps around his head and shoulders, and the inertia carries them both
over the bike. They grapple in the dust where they fall. Sealove pins her for a
second but she gives him a quick head butt and slips out of his grasp. She disap-
pears back into the desert behind the garage. Sealove sits up, swirling.

Sealove tries to catch his breath, peering out into the desert Zeusie disappeared
into. Softly, he says,

Sealove   And then the cops came.

Lights Dim.

Sealove moves to work on bike.

SCENE TWO

Sealove struggles with removing the burnt, shrunken tire off the rim. He has borrowed Lourdes' tire irons and screwdrivers. His hands are covered in ash, dirt and grease. He occasionally uses a little water on the tire to loosen it up; things are getting messy.

Zeusie pushes the cart up to Sealove, still struggling with the tire. He stops and watches her. She rummages in the parts cart for an electrical blanket. She gets it out and unfolds it on the ground, slowly. She methodically takes a chrome plate from the middle of the blanket, squirts oil onto it, and drinks from it. She gets it all over her face, she licks her chops. She offers it to Sealove, who accepts. He is about to drink when Lourdes enters.

Lourdes   Mastery of the tongue. That's what that animal wants. She's tryin a teach her body this immunity to the industrial hazards, the solvents, the petro-based cleaners, oil-based cleansers. She likes things that are lighter than water. Lighter than you, that's for sure.

Sealove   I thought so.

Lourdes   Bet ya did.

Lourdes takes away the chrome plate.

Lourdes   I was in New York once. Saw *Cats.*

Sealove laughs.

Lourdes   Fucking Cats. Think they're gonna age gracefully. The oily dignity, the wisdom of the ages. Makes people believe there's a heaven.

She drinks. Sealove drinks. He looks to her for more.

Lourdes   This old lady cat dies, goes up on a hydraulic, the white lights, pisses me off to no end. Takes a lot of money to go see and it'll piss off a person with a will of steel.

Sealove   Yeah.

pause.

Lourdes	You found 'nuther tire yet?
Sealove	I'm hitchin to Tucumcari tomorrow. They said they probably have a one-80 at Felipe's.
Lourdes	Heard that before.
Sealove	I'm in no rush.
Lourdes	Why not?
Sealove	Well. You know, I got nowhere to go really.
Lourdes	East coast people are always got somewhere to go. What you out here for anyway.
Sealove	I told ya, see the land. Let the land do the talking.
Lourdes	Bull–shit. Yr runnin. Is it the Law or did ya just break somebody's heart?

pause.

Sealove	We were engaged. We called it off. We're taking the summer off. I got the bike in Baltimore from a salvage yard out near the docks.
Lourdes	What's the rule about buyin a used bike?
Sealove	"One word...."
Both:	DON'T.
Sealove	It's been solid so far.
Lourdes	Jap steel? Don't kid yourself.
Sealove	Well, you're not supposed to set 'em on fire, either.
Lourdes	No, you are not.
Sealove	But this trip is open. I want to get my hands fucked up

in the engine. I want them to get toughened up by the chemicals it takes to clean an engine.

Lourdes   Carb spray dulls the senses. I wonder sometimes if that's what's wrong with Zeusie. You're better off deciding right now exactly how long you want to live.

He drinks. She drinks. Pause. They listen to the noise of the highway.

Sealove   It's up to me?

Lourdes   Sweet bejesus. TRUDY!! What did we say after the Harley Gang was in here last week?

Lourdes imitates Trudy.

Lourdes   *What?*

Lourdes   The Poker Run! Tell 'im. How'd they leave?

Lourdes   *Ohh, Well, shit, they was all in here, right, whole bar. And they was drinkin slow for a couple hours. I heard they was gonna do another Poker Run, you know. Benefit Easter Seals or sump'n. But then their leader stands up and goes "We're leavin'." Ho ho! I mean the President of the Club just gets up and goes like*

Trudy snaps her fingers.

             "Yo! We're leaving Now." And every single biker just like drank up. Maaannn, I always wanted to go out on a Poker Run.

Lourdes   I awwwwaaays wanted to go out of a Poker Run.

Lourdes   *I did. I always wanted to go....*

Lourdes   I Always wanted to ride with the big mean ol' bikers, on the back of a hog, wearin colors, I'd see God and Fate, just two bums on the side of the highway. I could pass them off on my fat loud hog, or at least on the back, riding bitch on some cool nazi biker's fat hog.

Lourdes	*God. I don't know....*
Lourdes	Well then, Trudy, you SHOULD go out on a Poker Run. You gotta get out of Darlene's Whirlaway Cantina one night and hit that road. Get upta Murdo one of these summers, they'd love ya at bike week. Sealove here has a Honda he can get ya for cheap.
Lourdes	*I don't ride no Honda.*
Sealove	It's not for sale.
Lourdes	So of course it's "Up to You."
Sealove	What?
Lourdes	You asked. You asked, "It's up to me?"
Sealove	Bad habit
Lourdes	*Man, I always wanted to go out on a Poker Run.*
Lourdes	Exactly! Who wouldn't?

SCENE THREE

Later, after Sealove has put the bike back together, relatively speaking. Cody, the State Trooper, enters on the scene.

Cody   Your name

Sealove   Sealove

Cody   Your occupation?   .

Sealove   Amateur fugitive

Cody   'Scuse Me?

Sealove   Writer

Cody   Let's start over. Your name?

Cody holds out his hand.

Sealove   Maddalena, Sealove

Sealove hands over his license.

Cody   Your occupation?

Sealove   Copier

Cody   Favorite drugs?

Sealove   Excuse me?

Cody   Do you do drugs?

Sealove   Let's start over. My name.

Cody   Oh come on man, you do a few drugs, you know, now
                and then?

pause.

Sealove	Yeah.
Cody	Favorite Drugs?
Sealove	Acid, shrooms, X...New York Buddha bud...brand...
Cody	Your name?
Sealove	Umm, Sealove
Cody	Your Occupation?
Sealove	Biker
Cody	Listen to yourself.
Sealove	Copier
Cody	What state is this thing registered in?
Sealove	Baltimore
Cody	That plate looks fake.
Sealove	It was on fire yesterday.
Cody	And you reported this to?
Sealove	Some government.
Cody	Right. OK, here we go, open all your bags.
Sealove	Excuse me?
Cody	Open 'em up. I'm going to have to search through all your stuff.
Sealove	I don't think that's reasonable.
Cody	You said you take drugs
Sealove	I thought You asked me that. I didn't know it was the

cop part of you.

Cody	You don't know me.
Sealove	It was CASUAL, informal, completely off the record.
Cody	Ok, here we go. Open 'em up.
Sealove	I'd like to know what reasonable justification....
Cody	Are you a lawyer?
Sealove	"There's no idea if it's not about freedom."—Hegel.
Cody	You're high! Pin your own arms behind your back.

Cody goes through Sealove's stuff.

Sealove	Where were you when I needed you? When I was rebuilding a carburetor in the rain outside Front Royal?
Cody	How did you rebuild a carburetor in the rain?
Sealove	OK, Cleaned it.

pause.

Sealove	A bit.
Cody	What kind of hat is this?
Sealove	Brooklyn.
Cody	Lenin
Sealove	What
Cody	You a communist?

pause.

Cody	You're not a communist are you?

Sealove	What does that word mean to you?
Cody	Marxist-Leninist. But don't worry, I'm not too politically correct myself.
Sealove	Now, what does that term mean to you?
Cody	Politically correct?
Sealove	Did you get that one new, or new-used?
Cody	Look Lenin, isn't there something about this country that to your face tells you Class Struggle is not the main problem?
Sealove	Sure. The Land doesn't need us.
Cody	The common man doesn't know anything about the stuff you talk about.
Sealove	The workers know me.
Cody	The babes don't
Sealove	I am the babe.

Zeusie pops up and gets on the bike. Caterwauling.

Zeusie	WALK LIKE A MAN
	JAM IT IN YOUR CAN
	TOUCH ME ON THE MOUTH
	GIVE YOURSELF A HAND.
	YOU WALK LIKE A MAN
	YOU MAKE LOVE TO YOUR HANDS
	YOU DON'T RUN WITH THE GOATS
	YOU ARE A SYSTEMS MAN

Cody goes to Zeusie. The Radio comes on from the offstage patrol car:

Dispatcher	Delta 241, we have confirmation of a New York license

	for a Sealove Maddalena, motorcycle endorsement, wears corrective lenses, Democrat last too elections,
Sealove	I can explain.
Dispatcher	Caucasian, well-nourished, admits to being in therapy in the past. Copy?
Cody	Copy.

Cody hands back the license.

Sealove	What is Zeusie?
Cody	No comment.
Sealove	If I could start over, I'd like to revise my first answer. For the record, I do do drugs, yes but only legal ones, certain painkillers the hospital back home gives me. I have a bad back.
Cody	Well-spoken. Step over here and place your hands on top of the car.

Cody frisks Sealove. Sealove laughs.

Cody	This funny to you?
Sealove	It tickles, sir.
Cody	Where do you sleep? In motels?
Sealove	Junkyards.

Cody finds something on Sealove.

Cody	Yep!
Sealove	That's a petrified dinosaur jaw bone. It was a gift from a junk dealer.
Cody	I bet it was. Junk. OK this is the way we're gonna run

this. You're gonna stay in this county tonight, on your own recognizance and in custody of the fact that you do do drugs; you told me you did. And you'll say But You Made It Seem Like A Casual Question. And I'll say don't tell me what style of conversation to use when I'm doing my job. And then I find something that looks just like a drug. Is it just another decoy? I'll have to wonder, "How stupid are you you tell me the truth when I ask you a simple question?"

Sealove   I didn't know what you expected from me. I thought "The Truth Will Set You Free."

Cody   No, covering your ass will set you free. Keeping your mouth shut will set you free.

Zeusie gets back on the bike. Sings to the tune of "Urgent" by Foreigner

Zeusie: SOMETIMES I WONDER
              WHEN I WANT A SURPRISE
              THAT MAYBE YOU'LL BAKE ME
              A MINCEMEAT PIE
              BUT I KNOW
              YES I KNOW
              THAT YOU'VE PETTED THE GOAT
              THAT'S WHY YOU REFUSE
              TO MAKE A PAYMENT ON THE BOAT.

Cody   I am paying off the Boat.

Zeusie   You RRRRR KNOT! YouRRR ReFuse. Payment. Boat. Payment.

Cody   Who told you about the boat?

Zeusie   Coming up next another 45 minutes of continuous non-stop Classic Rock. Bbmmmm.

Cody   Get down off of that thing now! Zeusie!!

Zeusie	BOAT!!

She starts the bike. She pops the clutch and jolts out onto the road. She's gone. Cody comes out and stares at the horizon with Sealove.

Sealove	Maaan, I just got done finally fixing that thing. If she wrecks, we'll never find her.

Cody	She's not gonna wreck.

Sealove	How the hell do you know?

Cody	Any body can see what happens out on a highway, a fire a wreck are for anyone.

He turns to go.

Sealove	You'd be in mourning?

Cody	I'm not an expert at expressing emotions in uniform.

Sealove	Your name?

Cody	State Highway Patrolman John Cody

Sealove	Your Occupation?

Cody	Ex-Quartback

Sealove	It's all power to you?

Cody	I have needs. Private, personal matters. I live on this planet, I gotta get satisfaction from some job, right?

Sealove shoots him a look, runs stage left to the ramp of the highway, stops at the No Pedestrians No Animals sign and sticks out his thumb.

SCENE FOUR

Inside the garage. Cody and Lourdes. Lourdes is standing behind the counter, leaning.

Lourdes   I thought I never told you to come back here.

Cody   I'm stupid.

Lourdes   You're so stupid.

Cody sings a bit of their favorite Hank Williams song, "Lonesome Blues" over the sound of the drill.

Cody   "SHE'LL DO ME
SHE'LL DO YOU
SHE'S GOT THAT KIND OF LOVIN'
LAWD I LOVE TO HEAR IT WHEN SHE CALLS ME
SWEET DAAAADYY."

Lourdes   I thought YOU were never comin back, that You didn't want to.

Cody   Maybe there's something between us undone yet.

Lourdes   Can't imagine what. I had no problems without you. I was teaching Zeusie to talk, my way. She wasn't goin off no highway. And I really liked cleaning all your shit our of my room.

Cody   Who taught Zeusie to ride?

Lourdes   Wasn't me.

Cody   There's somethin here someone's not sayin. I just don't get it. Have I just been outta the loop a little too long? I don't get either of you.

He gets up and puts on his hat.

Lourdes	That's it? You leave and it's a scam. I feel scammed every time.
Cody	You said you enjoyed my absence
Lourdes	I was making it easy on you just then
Cody	Well, I'm back now.
Lourdes	You don't deserve easy. You deserve hard as nails. Learn ya good.
Cody	I just want to be with you. Here in our place.
Lourdes	OUR Place? Your place is space.
Cody	Lourdes
Lourdes	There are a ton of other spaces, spaces wider. Maybe you'd be happier there.
Cody	I'm happy enough here
Lourdes	Just happy enough? You're like Zeusie. You don't listen to a thing I say.
Cody	"Can I get you another drink?" "No thanks, why don't we just go somewhere and fool around?" "Where do you want to go?"
Lourdes	Hows about "straight to hell?"

She leads him into her room, in the rear of the station.

SCENE FIVE

Inside a courtroom of the mind.

Sealove as Counsel for the Defendant. The defendant is Zeusie, who lies in a small coffin on Counsel's table. The audience is the jury.

Sealove   Your exalted highness, you can't condemn my experimental speed demon to hell. Despise not this petition. If you are God, and you look like God, look down on her lanky obscurity. Most merciful in all of show business, I ask you, bestow mercy here on the svelte forehead of the accused. "Accused of what, again?" the jury may ask? Death. We've heard wild accusations of terminus through speed. And who could have blamed her? Zeusie, like her namesake, found a validity in the impetuous, the power of these motorized bikes on long, rippled highways. The cracks swell into ridges, the 18-wheelers are slow, a two-lane only allows for a quick passing out of the path of on-coming traffic. Those cracks swell into little ramps, you are airborne for what? A second? A half-second? Anytime, anything could happen. Did the fire fry the wires? Is the wheel scored, warped? Did the fire fatigue the frame? Heat from four semi-oiled pistons at the core of this heart, heat from a sharp, boring sun, plus then, the final heat, the aggressive little ball of fire, a child born of polyester and a pukingly hot exhaust system. How can we find this creature anything but innocent? No, not just Not Guilty, but pure, and young, and dead?

Pause.

And in need of a paradise for her eternal soul?

SCENE SIX

3 AM, Outside of Lourdes's garage, Sealove wakes up. He is alone. He expects Zeusie to pop up from somewhere. Inside the garage, Lourdes and Cody fight while Cody is pulling on his clothes

Lourdes   You have no control!

Cody   I control you.

Lourdes   You have no handle on yourself

Cody   I have a power inside of you

Lourdes   You have no control inside of me.

Cody   I've been practicing

Lourdes   On who?

Cody   I was safe

Lourdes   On horses?

Cody   None of yours

Lourdes   You'll fall asleep right after anyway

Cody   Keep me up

Lourdes   You won't want to

Cody   Call the shots

Lourdes   Call a play?

Cody   This isn't a sport.

Lourdes   It's a game. I play fooling myself every time. I am not

"In Love" with you anymore. This is just a pattern we fall into.

Cody   Let's watch ourselves fall.

Lourdes   Won't that be a surprise?

Cody   I'll surprise you this time.

Lourdes   You'll come in two seconds. What is that the surprise? Men either rape for power and don't come, or else they lose it early, "In Love," coming like it's the "first time". Why can't you fuck for power?

She gets up. He sings.

Cody   "Feels like the first time. Feels like the very first time."

Lourdes   I have a will of steel now.

Cody   I can feel that.

Lourdes   I don't need you crude

Cody   Fight me.

Lourdes   We don't play that anymore

Cody   Oh c'mon. I thought you said I deserved hard as nails.

Lourdes   I'm not your spring chicken

Cody   It's okay. Fight me.

They wrestle each other back into bed. They grapple.

Sealove   Eyes on the road. No unnecessary risks as they say in the books...Of course that doesn't make sense. Show me a spot where the risk stops.

Zeusie, appears in half light on top of the garage.

Sealove   I mean, show me a spot where your cells are splitting
                 still, and things aren't stopping.

Zeusie rises up, reaches into her body, takes out her heart, extends it to Sealove.

Suddenly, Sealove has the heart in his hand.

Sealove   We're in an emergency situation. No time for tears.
                 Cusses? Sure. They might even help. My voice will
                 force my head to come up with the right reaction.

He stares down at the heart.

Sealove   FUCK!

Sealove, heart in hand, is looking up into the night sky.

Sealove   FUCK!

He stashes it into his jacket.

SCENE SEVEN

Dawn outside the garage Sealove wakes himself up violently.

Sealove   FUCK!

Lourdes comes over to him.

Lourdes   Got something for us in Tucumcari?

Sealove   What?

Lourdes   Got something for me?

Sealove   Something for the bike...

Lourdes   You got a BIKE?

Sealove	The Honda.
Lourdes	*high pitched, mocking*
	HonononononON-ON-ONNNDDDAAAA?

pause.

Sealove	Got a light?
Lourdes	Fuck smokes, you said you quit. Make you smell like highway trash, anyway.
Sealove	It's either freedom or its not.
Lourdes	What?
Sealove	Smoking. Is it something we do because we can, or because we started a little while ago?
Lourdes	Cody says Zeusie's disappeared. Know anything about that?
Sealove	But look at my arms. I feel the nicotine ache in my arms.
Lourdes	Where's your bike?
Sealove	What about acupuncture?
Lourdes	Fuck Acupuncture
Sealove	Well, you are electricity, you are nerves, you know that.
Lourdes	mmm.
Sealove	And there are concentrations of this electricity inside you....
Lourdes	Maybe
Sealove	And they get weaker or stronger like anything, the

moon, the tides...you try and quit smoking when you don't have the current for it....

Lourdes   I know. You get something started you gotta follow it through.

Sealove   You don't have to tell me

Lourdes   Boy your age not gonna be able to keep it up long.

Sealove   You might be surprised.

Lourdes   Probably not.

Sealove   Why not?

Lourdes   Fresh as the flowers.

Sealove   Toughened up by the megalopolis since birth

Lourdes   Unseasoned. Can't rig a saddle bag so it don't catch fire once 'e's out of the fog.

Sealove   I've changed tires, without getting taught.

Lourdes   Zeusie could change tires, WHEN SHE WAS ROUND HERE.

Sealove   I've torn two of those Honda engines down to their elements.

Lourdes   Bring her back up?

Sealove   If you are unsure of the metal, why don't you test it?

Lourdes   Why don't you ask your girlfriend in Tucumcari to test it? See how long...

Sealove   It was casual, informal, completely off the record. We were standing up for Christ's sake. Acupuncture. The bike is just like the body, see, electrical...

Lourdes   Sealove.

Sealove	What
Lourdes	I'm not saying this to you, you didn't hear it. Zeusie is one of a kind. There will never be another like her. I don't know what you did to her, what you know about her, but if you have anything, any clue as to where I can find her, how I can get her back, you tell me. Otherwise, I will get myself a real bike again, I will get out there on the trails, and I will TRACK you.

pause.

Sealove	I don't know the first thing in this town.

Cody comes out, in a work shirt. He's drinking beer.

Cody	Well
Sealove	Hey
Cody	Hey?

pause.

Cody	She tell you?
Sealove	What
Cody	She was worried
Lourdes	hah.
Cody	We were wondering where you were.
Sealove	Long road.
Cody	Yeah...
Sealove	I broke down

Cody	Yeah…
Sealove	Breakdowns take a while
Cody	Especially when you try and rebuild a carburetor in the rain outside "Front Royal?"
Sealove	Exactly
Cody	You ever worked on bikes before?

pause.

	You don't know what the FUCK you're doing. Anybody can take a bike a fucking part. You got the Manual? You got the Clymer's? I bet its just covered with your greasy thumb prints by now. Makes you look like a real mechanic, huh? You get to that one page yet, "How to Fix a Major Fuck-Up?"
Sealove	It's not fucked-up.
Cody	No, I think you're the fuck-up. New York boys like to get fucked up, right?
Sealove	You wanna know, huh?
Cody	I'm not saying that.
Sealove	The body is sensitive in ways we've forgotten.
Cody	"We" didn't forget anything.
Sealove	Even with women, there's can be an erotic in that sphincter, the "asshole," your prostate is a bundle of nerves, so…
Cody	I am an officer of the law, I'd advise you to…
Sealove	…Not always "penetration." I'm talking about an open-ended, flavor-seeking probing. Improve your life.

Cody grabs Sealove by the collar and pulls him close to his face.

Cody	Truckstop boywhore.
Sealove	I'm the epitome of civilization. I'm the most advanced model we've produced yet.
Lourdes	You're Grunge, right?
Sealove	I'm Punk.
Lourdes	You need to either tell me what happened to Zeusie or you need to get out of here. This is your summer off, huh?

Sealove silent.

Sealove	Well, do I break up with her?
Lourdes	You need to do what you're trying to do. You're not the one in prison.
Sealove	Is that where Zeusie is?
Lourdes	No. I checked already. But it wouldn't'a been the first time she was inside.
Sealove	If she was inside, I'd want spring her.
Lourdes	Oh, that's nice. Baby's learning the language of convicts.
Sealove	What is she guilty of?
Lourdes	What are you, Pontius Pilate?
Sealove	Who?
Lourdes	The Roman who washed his hands instead a judging Jesus Christ. I got it tatooed on my left deltoid. Show ya next time you come through.
Sealove	Why is...

Lourdes	Used to be my riding name. Harley gang, you would-n't....Hey you know what you're riding name would be?
Sealove	What?
Lourdes	Economy Denture Center.

She laughs. Then, after a pause.

Lourdes	You don't get the summer off. Cody, let him go.

SCENE EIGHT

It is early morning. Sealove's bike is back in front of the garage. In the same condition that Zeusie stole it in. Sealove is lashing the last of his bags onto the bike.

Cody	You're going to need one of these.

He produces a new license plate for Sealove.

Sealove	I'm blown away.
Cody	Got twenty bucks?
Sealove	Oh, you're too good.
Cody	Good?
Sealove	You want it to be a valueless gesture. Thanks, I'll take it. I need it to finish the trip.
Cody	You have a certain fate, then, after all.
Sealove	If I do, It's certainly not here. Just get out of the waste-land I used to purr into this engine when it was failing. I don't understand you, but I can always go deeeper into you.
Cody	Don't

Sealove   I don't. I just waste time prying big things off and on.
               Burning and replacing, like tires.

Cody   If you hadn't had that fire, I'm sure something worse
               would have hit you down the road. It's all for the best.

*Sealove gets on. He adjusts the petticock, the choke. He's on the center stand. He
starts it. He takes off.*

SCENE NINE

*Inside a tiny office in the back of a Taco Bell. Manager is big, shirt is small, sitting
in a swivel chair. Zeusie is sitting in front of him.*

Manager   Stress. Pressure! The customers demand perfection
               every time. You're making the tacos. Or a bean burrito.
               Beans, Lettuce, Sauce. Beans, Lettuce, Sauce. You feel
               the tension in your neck. You hear their voices behind
               you. That's stress. Some people think stress is an
               abstract thing, that's their first mistake. Stress is physi-
               cal. It's very physical.

Zeusie   Yes

Manager   You understand

Zeusie   Yes

Manager   You've had experiences with stress?

Zeusie   Yes

Manager   Lots of stress?

Zeusie   Yes!

Manager   I mean something SPECIAL. That's what we're looking
               for, here. People that are special.

Zeusie	YES! Yes. umm. um. Yes.
Manager	OK. Oookay. Yes. Well we'll go ahead and give you a shot. Second shift. Tomorrow. Show up at 3 for training you start at 4. Oh, one last thing, you have experience with machines?
Zeusie	Yes.

Zeusie gets up. Manager extends hand. Zeusie just looks at it. Five seconds pass.

SCENE TEN

Zeusie is in a uniform, mopping at the Taco Bell. Softly, she is singing "Magic Man," and using the right words.

Zeusie	COME ON HOME, GIRL
	HE SAID WITH A SMILE
	YOU DON'T HAVE TO LOVE ME
	LET'S JUST GET HIGH A WHILE
	BUT TRY AND UNDERSTAND
	TRY AND UNDERSTAND
	TRY TRY TRY and understaaand.
	HE'S A MAGIC MAN.
	HE'S A MAA HAA GIC MAN.
	HE'S A MAGIC maaaaaHAAAAAAANNN aaYAAAAaan.
	HE'S A MAGIC MAN, MOMMA.

SCENE ELEVEN

At Taco Bell, later. Sealove enters with his helmet in his hands. He has been riding all day and is pretty whipped. Zeusie is waiting patiently behind the counter. Sealove is staring blindly into the price board, swaying slightly, wind-burnt.

Zeusie   You been riding far on your motorbike?

He looks quickly at her, dismissively.

Zeusie   How far?

Sealove   Can I get a coffee black, large, please?

Zeusie   How far?

She does nothing. He stops sees this.

Zeusie   How far?

Sealove   back. east.

Zeusie   Yeah.

Sealove   I'll take the little creams on the side.

She slowly places them on the steel counter. He pops them into his mouth.

Zeusie   Really I think that's smart you know, keeping to your-
                self.

Sealove   You asked.

Zeusie   No, my Friend always used to say, you don't just Tell
                Anyone where you're going, where you been. None of
                their business if you don't know 'em. Plus, well, another
                reason.

Sealove   Thanks.

He turns to go.

Zeusie	Let's see if I can figure this thing out. punches one button on the register. Oh yeah. Seventy Eight Cents. Pleeese.

He stops, turns around, digs up and gives her the change.

Zeusie	You from a Big City back East?
Sealove	What would your "friend" say.
Zeusie	Oh, he wouldn't mind tellin' some fast food worker nothing.
Sealove	He wouldn't?
Zeusie	No no. He was talkin bout people in Society. You know. Adults.
Sealove	You're not an adult?
Zeusie	Plus, there's another reason. The one I didn't get to just now.
Sealove	What.
Zeusie	COPS! If you tell everyone who you are, and where you're going, and you look, you know, SUSPICIOUS, people will have more to mention. The cops will be more likely to pull you over later.
Sealove	That a fact?
Zeusie	"Yeah, they were travelling in a RV together. They looked like a couple of those posters in the post office. One of them was in a, in a A FAST FOOD UNIFORM. The other was scruffy and mean-lookin'. They was on Drugs, I can tell ya."
Sealove	"No officer, I'm married, separated, got three kids."
Zeusie	Get That Guy!

Sealove	"I got so sick of the alimony to the ungrateful bitch, I just had to, I mean, this ain't what it looks like, some joyride out here. I'm runnin'. And I shore could use a break. You understand, right?"
Zeusie	I Don't Understand Anything! You could use some Time INSIDE!!
Sealove	You Don't KNOW Me!

small pause

Zeusie	They'll shore be sore when they come in askin' after you.
Sealove	and what'll you tell 'em?
Zeusie	Nothin. Just that he was a no-good LIAR.

nose to nose.

Sealove	Then I'll have to come in here and wring you neck, kid.
Zeusie	I'm older than you, kid.
Sealove	Age don't matter. Age don't make one bit of difference.
Zeusie	No, I think age does make a difference. I lied. I'm not older than you.

she steps back a little and grins.

	More Coffee?
Sealove	Thanks.

SCENE TWELVE

Sealove and a blond mechanic named Ken are listening to the engine.

Ken	You hear that?
Sealove	Um. Wait. I think so.
Ken	Over here.
Sealove	The high pitch?
Ken	That thoop thoop thoop?
Sealove!	Yeah!
Ken	Bent valve.
Sealove	Great! How do I fix it?

Ken hits the kill switch.

Ken	You don't. You replace the whole thing.
Sealove	mmm.
Ken	What do you want to do?
Sealove	I just don't have the money.
Ken	Well I'll tell you, this engine's got about another five hundred miles. If you're lucky.

SCENE THIRTEEN

Sealove is staring up at the price board. Sealove is increasingly exhausted from the road. Zeusie is waiting patiently on his order.

Sealove   Yeah could I get a...black coffee...large?

Zeusie   Aren't you gonna ask me what MY dreams are?

Sealove   No.

Zeusie   Now, I don't think that's very fair.

Sealove   I'll take the little creams on the side.

Zeusie   It's not fair you comin in here every day and night, talkin bout yer little DREAM, buyin some land gonna give up the booze and the one night stands but never once thinking Hey, ThinKinG HEY! Maybe that retarded looking kid with the tacos has some dreams too!

pause.

Sealove   Please, I'm looking for someone. I've been searching for weeks. I'm running out of money. And today...I learned my engine....

Zeusie   Well maybe I HAVE some dreams.

Sealove   I'm sure you have some.

Zeusie   Be quiet. Ask me now. And say "kid." Call me "kid."

Sealove   I'm a loner. I'm more of a loner than you think I am.

Zeusie   I don't think you're anyone. I don't know you from any other post office poster.

Sealove   I am moving through here so totally solo. If you don't always keep that in mind, that fact, that you're moving alone, this highway will rise up and strip you down. You will be humiliated. So I'm moving.

Zeusie   I know. My daddy's a cop. He comes home sometimes
          and finds candles are burning in the apartment. And I
          don't live there anymore. Nobody will be there for like
          eight hours, and he sees the candles and then later he
          says like, he says, "Hey! You haven't been lighting can-
          dles in my apartment while I was out stopping taxi-cabs
          and looking inside them, were ya?"

Sealove   500 miles and then it's all over for this engine. I am
          moving out. Now.

Zeusie   You'll want more coffee first.

Sealove   I WILL NOT want more Fucking coffee. WHO MAKES
          THIS STUFF?

He walks out the door. He turns back and yells from the other side of the glass.

          LOOK AT ME, KID. I AM ALONE.

He bangs on the glass.

          HA HA HA! LOOK AT ME.

*Zeusie ignores Sealove yelling and banging on the glass. Zeusie is whistling to her-
self and wiping the counter with a pretty rag.*

SCENE FOURTEEN

Sealove has been pulled over, lights are flashing. Sealove sits on the bike.

Cody   Let's have your real license this time, Matt.

Sealove   Is Zeusie back? I need to make a decision. And I want
          your influence.

Cody   Let me scan this first.

Sealove	I want an answer.
Cody	Hold on, Tex.

Sealove sits in the headlights for a little while.

Cody	A ha. You've changed your party affiliations since we last talked.
Sealove	Is Zeusie here?
Cody	Good. That's good.
Sealove	Is Zeusie dead? I'm not picking up any trace of her out here.
Cody	You're a goddam riot, is Zeusie dead. No concept of death, candy-ass.
Sealove	The cat is not around.
Cody	The cat is not dead. She didn't wreck your bike, did she? I would know. When you go, that's your time to go. You can't get out of the way of the bullet with your name on it. Remember that next time you give me a fake ID.
Sealove	It wasn't fake. It was real. It just wasn't the real me. It's okay if you want to influence me. I need help.
Cody	You letting the moment pass you by.
Sealove	Zeusie never spoke English. How far can she get in this country.
Cody	How close are we to the border?
Sealove	Maybe that's what I should go. Cross into Mexico and rest. Settle down. Get a job fixing motorcycles. Get good at being a real mechanic.
Cody	Lourdes is a mechanic, you're just a communist. You're not even a real communist.

Sealove	I'm both things.
Cody	Well you can't be both things.
Sealove	When I wanted to grow up I wanted to be a Cowboy and an Indian plus a Gold Miner.
Cody	Well you're not going to grow up anymore after this, okay? Try and learn from what's going on, instead of being above it all. You don't have to be from one of those rotten old cities to be able to speak about something. Here the people are decent, see? Know when to open their mouths, when not to.
Sealove	The more I get stopped, the more questions I'm asked.
Cody	In a minute, it's going to be "What are your last words."
Sealove	In a minute, it's going to be, "Do you have a cigarette?"
Cody	It's gonna be, "Didn't you quit?"
Sealove	It's gonna be, "Why should I when I'm about to be executed?"
Cody	You feel threatened?
Sealove	There's a real question. Here's a real answer. Of course I'm threatened. You get near me and the power paranoia that makes you you, that made you want to become a cop, wears off. It gets ON me.
Cody	Come on Matt, you're talking to me. Officer Cody. See past my reserved exterior, my contained manners, my tools and belts, see my voraciously hungry little person. Am I just a cop?
Sealove	No more questions, your honor.
Cody	My name is Cody. I have a natural curiosity.

Sealove	Well you shouldn't have become a cop, Officer Cody.
Cody	Well, I'm a cop.
Sealove	Then stick to the fucking Cop questions. And let me go eventually. Please.
Cody	If that's what was done who would want to be a cop?
Sealove	Dogs
Cody	Son, you got a mouth.
Sealove	No, when a dog is in a play, back in New York, everyone cheers when it sits down on stage, just because it's cute, but even more because it's well-behaved. Only dogs should be cops.
Cody	Some dogs are. Drive safely.

He hands Sealove his license.

SCENE FIFTEEN

Taco Bell at night, Zeusie and Sealove play at the counter.

Sealove	I'm a millionaire
Zeusie	OKay.
Sealove	I'm in advertising. I live in New York City.
Zeusie	Uh huh.
Sealove	I'm casually cruel to the well-dressed urban middle class of professional sufferers I gather underneath me. I'm a talent. I can insult my graphic design servants without even thinking about it. Some of them think I'm testing them, they look at their italian shoes, and are grateful.

Zeusie	Shh Shh Who am I?
Sealove	You're not one of the testees, at least not yet. You're back there, behind the counter. You're the copier.
Zeusie	So my life is in transition, or am I in a rut?
Sealove	Maybe you were born to be a copier.
Zeusie	Maybe I wasn't educated properly. Maybe no one ever taught me to speak.
Sealove	It doesn't matter to me. I don't know your name. I don't plan on learning it.
Zeusie	I'm waiting for the day maybe when the electricity goes out because?
Sealove	Maybe a revolution happens. A bloody one.
Zeusie	and the elevators are stuck.
Sealove	Yes. Let's put everyone in the agency together in the dim, 66-person capacity freight elevator.
Zeusie	There are no elevators that big.
Sealove	Oh yes there are, Kid. Welcome to SoHo. Welcome to the chrome, vacuous, elegant space of my power.
Zeusie	OKAY. Be quiet.

Zeusie hops over the counter. She whips Sealove with her pretty rag. He falls to his knees.

Zeusie	It's time now for MY takeover. I corner you in the elevator. I grip your rolls of flesh. You are FAT! I scream. You are FAT!
Sealove	I prefer "bon-vivante."
Zeusie	How is it that I fear a man who couldn't sell a fragrance-

licensing deal to Slyvester Stallone?

Sealove   No one remembers that!

Zeusie   I'm the copier! Your copier baby, and I'm reading everything I see. Don't worry Slim, you're not gonna die, not
yet. Think of this as a new kind of lawsuit. I won't cut you
open in front of your staff, if only you let me tell you I
remember everything. I know more about you than
comes to mind right now, to your own mind.

Sealove   But I'm a millionaire. I'm sure there's a way we could
reach an understanding....

Zeusie   OOoohhh, you little animal, come here. C'mere Big Guy
how about a HUG, huh?

*Sealove grabs Zeusie around the knees, and weeps for mercy, intuitively, for
everything he doesn't recognize.*

SCENE SIXTEEN

Sealove gets pulled over again.

Cody   Two charges

Sealove   Why two charges?

Cody   You failed to yield.

Sealove   I yielded

Cody   I was driving for a good while behind you, at least two
minutes. This time I'm writing you up.

Sealove   Maybe I just wasn't checking my mirrors, I yielded
when I saw it was you.

Cody   Two charges. Speeding, and Failure to Yield.

Sealove	But I'm a millionaire.
Cody	You're not talking anymore.
Sealove	It was all a question of just concentrating. I became a millionaire.
Cody	Drinking and driving is a serious crime, Matt. Do the crime, you'll do the time.
Sealove	But what about the value of a dollar?
Cody	You're a Marxist-Leninist.
Sealove	But what I am is a millionaire.
Cody	So why'd you stop and pull over?
Sealove	To have this conversation. To arrange a date in court. To tempt myself: maybe I could tackle you, and take your gun... Ha Ha! A joke!

pause.

Cody	Because you're really a millionaire?

Cody turns away to go. Sealove sneaks off the bike, silently grabs Cody's pistol from behind.

Sealove	Don't you believe it.

He grabs Cody by the throat, and smashes his head on the bike. Cody struggles but Sealove has the gun trained on his face. Sealove crushes his throat. Sealove was hoping he wouldn't have to shoot him, and for a moment is glad it could happen a little more gracefully. But he's not only glad. He's falling apart.

Sealove enters the Taco Bell with a big brown army body bag strapped onto the back of his bike. He parks on the center stand. Get's off, unbunjees the bag, and hikes it up on a shoulder. He walks through the glass doors of the Taco Bell. It is just he and Zeusie, alone, in the abandoned local fast food franchise.

Zeusie   So I said to this girl in here, I'd like to see you try. I said I'd like to see you try. Knock this purple towel here offa my shoulder.

Sealove   The market bears it. This, I mean.

He sets the bag down on the steel counter.

Zeusie   oh. um...really?

Sealove   You're not going to get in trouble.

Zeusie   I am not thinking about trouble anymore. I've got much bigger problems with things in here, now.

Zeusie touches her head. Sealove unzipps and pulls away the bag. He begins to prepare the body of Cody for burial preparations, between the registers.

Sealove   The market pays top dollar, get it? Undercut the selling of noxious ground gristle patties with beans or kill police officers because otherwise you have no dreams. The market is everything, it's you and me. It IS Discipline.

Zeusie   So I said to this girl in here, go ahead. You're not in love with him anymore anyhow. So go ahead, he's the one on the road. And all she could say was, "Coming up next a Forty Minute Rock Block on the new Q Q AMERICA AMERICA AMERICA. I AM BEING STRANGLED ALIVE. I AM MADE OF MORE THAN JUST CLASSIC ROCK. I AM NOT IN LOVE WITH YOU ANYMORE. YOU'RE THE ONE THAT CALLED IT OFF. go ahead knock this purple towel offa my shoulder. Then the music started, and then we'll walk down the light blue hall way, and then we cha-cha-chaed.

Sealove	Say "Bitch."
Zeusie	bitch
Sealove	No, it's so beneath you, You'd have to be someone else first and say, "bitch." Be someone else and say "bitch."
Zeusie	bitch.
Sealove	Continue your story.
Zeusie	So I said to this girl. in here. I'd like. To see you try...
Sealove	Take his body for ten dollars.
Zeusie	Call me kid.
Sealove	Yo Kid.
Zeusie	FIVE
Sealove	Wait...do you want to pay less or do I?
Zeusie	You don't remember? Well dude...
Sealove	Dude, don't dude me.
Zeusie	Dude...
Sealove	dude.

slight pause.

Zeusie	You want me to pay more, but I don't want to pay more
Sealove	Right! TEN DOLLARS.
Zeusie	And I go, "five."
Sealove	And I go TEN DOLLARS

Zeusie	Dude
Sealove	Dude, don't dude me.
Zeusie	Dude.
Sealove	Dude, don't dude me.
Zeusie	Dude
Sealove	OKAY!!! FIVE!

Sealove reaches for his wallet, but Zeusie gets a $5 bill out of the register first.

Sealove	Wait. There's one thing I want.

He takes the pistol.

Zeusie	Call me kid. Call me kid.
Sealove	Grind him into the beans.
Zeusie	I will
Sealove	Don't save his badge, or his ID shit, and if you do, don't leave it lying around.
Zeusie	Right, right.
Sealove	Repeat back to me what I just said.
Zeusie	Dude.

Sealove walks into Lourdes' garage at night.

Lourdes   Where's the bike?

Sealove   It exploded.

He puts down his bags.

                 You ever see a valve try and come out of the head?

Lourdes   not pretty, I suppose.

Sealove   un-uh.

Lourdes   Any trace of Zeusie

Sealove   I kept beginning to pick up traces, almost a trail. But I
                 kept running into trouble. I'm thinking bout heading
                 South, now.

Lourdes   They'd eat you alive down there.

Sealove   Come with me.

Lourdes   I got a commitment to this business.

Sealove   Yeah.

Lourdes   You don't care one way or the other.

Sealove   I'm just not saying I do if I do.

Lourdes   C'mere

*He comes closer. She grabs him by the jacket, pulls him closer, stops, puts her
hand inside his jacket. She comes out with Cody's pistol. She looks at it.*

Sealove   He said, tell her to keep an eye on the way the birds fly.

Lourdes   Where'd you see him?

Sealove   The Taco Bell in Tucumcari. We were both trying to
                 track Zeusie, our paths crossed there.

She is staring at him hard. She deliberately takes out and flicks out the Eagle knife.

Lourdes   Can I cut you a little bit? You'll like it.

Sealove   No

She walks behind him and slowly runs a finger along his neck.

Lourdes   Please.

She runs both her hands up his back, under his shirt.

Sealove   Ok, but if I tell you to stop, stop.

Lourdes   Sure.

She takes off his shirt, from behind him. She helps him twist it around his wrists.
She locks a chain to the wrists and shirt to hold it there.

Lourdes   been thinkin a lot about the word fatality.

Sealove   Yeah?

She cuts him lightly across the back with the knife.

Lourdes   Where'd you think they got that word?

Sealove pause.

Sealove   Fate?

Lourdes   Yeeaapp.

She cuts him again, diagonally, across the back. She steps back and admires her
work.

Lourdes   What do you think they were trying to tell us, when they invented life like this?

Sealove   That when you die, it's supposed to happen.

Lourdes   Yupp.

She cuts.

Lourdes   You wanna tell me what happened to Zeusie?

Sealove   I don't know.

Lourdes   Cody?

Sealove   mmm.

Lourdes   Are they together somewhere?

Sealove   No.

She holds the knife close to his neck.

Lourdes   How is it you know that?

Sealove   If I tell you to stop, will you stop?

Lourdes   I'd stop right now if't'd get me a straight answer.

Sealove   Straight off snuffed. I snuffed him like he was love
                 itself and I was anything else. Your love is dead. Or
                 your ex-love is xed, however you like.

She cuts him even more deliberately, slowly.

Sealove   I thought I asked you.

Lourdes   You thought about asking me.

Sealove   To stop.

Lourdes   Feels good, don't it?

Sealove	I'm leaking oil
Lourdes	Well, now you smoke
Sealove	I quit
Lourdes	You sure did
Sealove	I am so lazy when I'm lit
Lourdes	Big man. Did you shoot him?
Sealove	I was able, I was...I strangled him
Lourdes	What was that supposed to prove.
Sealove	That he wasn't a nice person
Lourdes	And he deserved to die?
Sealove	If someone was inspired enough.
Lourdes	Do you want to die?
Sealove	No, of course not.
Lourdes	Then why are you sitting there?

Sealove tries to get up, but he is woozy with the loss of blood.

Sealove	I love...I love....
Lourdes	Your love is candy. I know your kind.

CURTAIN.

"Sander Hicks has a band called White Collar Crime, but he has a blue collar job. He is a superintendent of an apartment building on Manhattan's Lower East Side, and he runs Soft Skull Press out of the basement. He has published 42 books so far, written five plays, and he's down with every cause on the Lower East Side, from urban gardens, to fighting gentrification, to squatting, to police harassment. And he's only 28 years old. So watch out."

—WILLIAM UPSKI WIMSATT
No More Prisons

Thanks

To all the people who have worked at Soft Skull:
Cat Tyc, Don Goede, Stuart Bagwell, Karla Zounek, Kris Mielen & Susan Mitchell;

To the Soft Skull writers William Upski Wimsatt, John S. Hall, Todd Colby, Cynthia Nelson, and especially Sparrow, who taught me so much about minimalism;

To my parents, who worked hard, sacrificed, tough-loved, and took me to the theater;

To my agent, Morgan Jenness;

To Richard Nash, the constantly attentive director, the excellent manager, the pioneering writer and great friend;

and finally to New Dramatists, who somehow still believe in the art of writing new plays in a age hostile to them.